SELF-HARMING PARROTS and Exploding TOADS

A marvellous compendium of bizarre, gross and stupid animal antics

Francesca Gould and David Haviland

piatkus

PIATKUS

First published in Great Britain in 2010 by Piatkus
Copyright © 2010 by Francesca Gould and David Haviland
The moral right of the authors has been asserted

A CIP catalogue record for this book is available from the British Library

ISBN 978-0-7499-5270-9

Cover and inside illustrations by Andrew Wightman
Designed and typeset in ITC Stone Serif by Paul Saunders
Printed in the UK by CPI Mackays, Chatham, ME5 8TD

Papers used by Piatkus are natural, renewable and recyclable
products sourced from well-managed forests and certified
in accordance with the rules of the Forest Stewardship Council.

Mixed Sources
Product group from well-managed
forests and other controlled sources
www.fsc.org   Cert no. SGS-COC-004081
© 1996 Forest Stewardship Council

FSC

Piatkus
An imprint of
Little, Brown Book Group
100 Victoria Embankment
London EC4Y 0DY

An Hachette UK Company
www.hachette.co.uk

www.piatkus.co.uk

SELF-HARMING
PARROTS
and
Exploding
TOADS

For Mum

Contents

	Acknowledgements	viii
CHAPTER ONE	Amazing animals	1
CHAPTER TWO	Peculiar parents	32
CHAPTER THREE	Crafty creatures	54
CHAPTER FOUR	Beastly blunders	83
CHAPTER FIVE	Filthy fauna	110
CHAPTER SIX	Sexy species	138
CHAPTER SEVEN	Vicious varmints	162
CHAPTER EIGHT	Weird wonders	184
	Index	211

Acknowledgements

The authors would like to thank our wonderful, dedicated literary agent, Andrew Lownie, for making this book happen. We also thank our editor, Andrew John, for professionalism and attention to detail which have gone a long way to covering up our own deficiencies in these areas. Many thanks to Claudia Dyer, Helen Stanton and all the team at Piatkus. Finally, we thank our families, for their continuing patience, support and encouragement.

CHAPTER ONE

Amazing animals

Which octopus is an expert impressionist?

There is a species of octopus that's able to mimic an incredible range of other sea life. It's a small, brown and white, mottled mollusc called the mimic octopus, which is about 60 centimetres (2 feet) long, and is found in the waters around Indonesia. It can change its colour and shape to resemble much of the local fauna. Many types of octopus can change colour, and some are even believed to be able to mimic one single other species, but the mimic octopus is the first known animal of any kind that can morph into a number of different physical impersonations in this way.

It can mimic at least fifteen other species, including sea snakes, lionfish, flatfish, sole fish, brittle stars, giant crabs, sea stars, stingrays, flounders, jellyfish, sea anemones and mantis shrimps. For example, it impersonates a sea snake by stuffing seven of its arms into a hole, and waving the remaining one in the water. It impersonates lionfish by hovering above the ocean floor with its arms spread out, trailing from its body, just like the lionfish's poisonous fins. Its impression of a sole consists of building up speed through jet propulsion, and drawing its arms in so that its body forms a flat wedge, which undulates just like the flat body of a sole.

This talent seems to be useful in two particular ways. Firstly, the mimic octopus uses this skill to get closer to its prey. For example, it will pretend to be a female crab, so as to get closer to an amorous male crab, which it will then grab and eat. It also uses mimicry to scare off its own predators. Most of the species it mimics are poisonous, and the octopus has the incredible ability to tailor its impressions to the intended audience, ensuring that it mimics the creature that will be most likely to discourage or scare off the predator. For example, when approached by a damselfish, a mimic octopus will suddenly appear to turn into a banded sea snake, which is a known predator of damselfish.

If you cut an earthworm in half, do you end up with two worms?

No, if you cut an earthworm in half, all you will usually end up with is two halves of a dead worm. Like most creatures, an earthworm cut in half will probably die. The only way it might survive is if the cut is made behind the thickest part of the worm, which is called the saddle, where all its major organs are found. If all of these organs are retained, the worm may manage to survive, since it should be able to regenerate a new anus. However, if the cut is made anywhere in front of the saddle, the earthworm is certain to die.

However, there is one type of worm that will form two new worms if cut in half. A planarian is a type of flatworm that's found in many parts of the world, in saltwater, freshwater, and on land. Amazingly, a planarian can be cut across its width or its length, and both halves will regenerate as a living worm. The reason this is possible is that flatworms have very simple body structures, with none of the complex organs that an earthworm requires to survive.

Which animal has been most useful in human warfare?

Animals have played a crucial role in the conduct of warfare for thousands of years. As you might guess, horses have been the most widely used animals throughout the history of warfare. Different types of horse have been used for an incredible range of purposes, including cavalry charges, communications, raiding, supplies and reconnaissance. Riders have fought on horseback using weapons as diverse as bows, javelins, swords, spears, lances, rifles and pistols.

The legendary military commander Hannibal was a keen exponent of the virtues of animal battalions. He gained a significant victory against the Romans during the Second

Punic War by tying flaming torches to the horns of enormous herds of cattle, and then sending them stampeding into the enemy's camp. Following this dramatic success, he decided to go even bigger, and recruited an army of elephants. The elephants were used successfully in a number of battles, but they were difficult to control, and they reacted badly to cold weather. Hannibal then famously tried to lead 37 elephants across the freezing cold Alps and into Rome, but the cold was insufferable, and most of the elephants died en route. Elephants can also be extremely useful for carrying heavy loads over difficult terrain, and were even used during World War Two by both Japan and the Allies.

The Romans came up with their own bizarre response to the threat of elephants, by using incendiary pigs. Pliny the Elder described a method of covering the pigs in tar, setting them alight, and sending them charging towards the enemy. The idea was that the squealing, flaming pigs would unsettle the enemy's elephants and horses, causing them to flee in panic.

In South Africa in the early 1800s, something extraordinary happened at a battle between two rival chieftains. One army was marching along, when the enemy suddenly appeared as if from nowhere, rising out of the centre of the earth. In fact, they had been hiding in enormous underground tunnels, which had been built by giant earthworms.

During World War Two, the American military were seriously considering using what became known as a 'bat bomb'. The idea was to fit millions of bats with tiny bombs, and drop them in Japanese airspace. The bats would naturally scatter and find somewhere to roost, often in the eaves and rafters of the enemy's homes, which tended to be built of wood. At a given time, the bombs would go off, simultaneously setting hundreds of thousands of fires. However, the first test run managed to burn a brand-new American airfield to the ground, and the idea was ditched.

In the same war, the Soviet army found a way to use dogs as anti-tank weapons. The dogs would be kept hungry, and trained to run under tanks to look for food. When used in the field, the dogs would have a bomb attached to them, which would be detonated by a small lever on their back. When the dog ran under the tank, this would trip the lever, detonating the bomb.

However, the scheme was not thought to be a great success. First, the dogs had been trained using Soviet tanks, and so often it would be their own side's tanks that they would run under, and destroy, rather than those of their intended German victims. Second, the dogs were often scared by the noise and chaos of the battlefield, and so would simply run away.

Sea lions are immensely intelligent, and are often trained to perform in circuses, water parks and zoos. Their intelligence has also been noted by the US Navy, who have trained these clever animals to help protect their ships in hostile waters. The sea lions are taught to swim behind any enemy diver they spot approaching a ship, and attach a clamp to his leg. Apparently, the sea lions are so quiet and nimble they can attach a clamp in seconds, without the diver even noticing their approach. The clamp is attached to a rope, allowing sailors to pull the diver on board, and interrogate him.

However, one could argue that the most useful creature in all of human warfare has been the humble carrier pigeon. During World War Two, more than half a million pigeons were conscripted into service. They were packed into tiny parachutes and dropped into occupied enemy areas, where they were gathered up and kept in rooks. When its time came, a pigeon would have a message taped to its leg, and would then be released to do what came naturally, which was of course to return home. The message would arrive back at the home base, and acted on accordingly.

One particular pigeon, which was given the name GI Joe, became something of a celebrity, after saving the lives of a thousand British troops. On 18 October 1943, a British brigade prepared to attack the Italian city of Colvi Vecchia. The plan was that a US bombing raid would damage the city's defences, and then the British would finish the job. But the German troops who were guarding the city retreated before the bombing, allowing the British to enter the city early.

However, the bombing raid was still planned, and there were no communication lines with which to send word to the Americans to cancel it. Thankfully, a trusty pigeon was on hand. GI Joe was sent with this crucial instruction, and arrived at the US airbase just in time. Afterwards, the commander of the US Fifth Army, General Mark Clarke, commented, 'GI Joe saved the lives of at least a thousand British allies.'

Which creature builds itself a refrigerated larder?

Many mammals that live in cold climates are forced to hibernate in winter, because a lack of available food requires them to conserve as much heat and energy as possible. However, beavers have an amazing way of surviving the winter, without having to sleep through and miss out on all the fun. They build themselves an underwater, refrigerated larder, which provides them with a constant supply of fresh, nutritious food throughout the winter, even when the woods around them are barren and covered with snow.

When setting up home for the first time, a pair of beavers will choose a valley with a small stream running through it. Across this stream, they build a dam. Beavers are big, powerful creatures, which can grow to four feet in length, and have enormous, sharp teeth. With these, they cut down trees and drag them into place on the stream bed. This construction is supported with rocks, and then plastered with mud on the upstream side. On the downstream side, more tree trunks are laid lengthways up against the dam wall, to provide support against the increasing weight of the water. Gradually, the lake behind the dam begins to swell, so the beavers respond by lengthening the dam. As this process continues, they may even use up all the nearby trees, and have to travel long distances to find more. Beavers sometimes even build canals, to transport wood down to their dam. A pair of beavers may maintain their dam for years, with some dams eventually becoming more than a hundred yards long.

Once the dam is built, the beavers start work on their underground lodge, where they will spend the winter. This will either be on the edge of the lake, or preferably on an island, for added security. The beavers build a tunnel which opens on the surface of the island, and leads down to a second, underwater entrance. They then cover the land entrance with rocks, branches, and mud, and then excavate the inside of the mound, creating a large, hollow chamber. They are now extremely safe, since their underground chamber is secure from above, and they can slip into the water unseen.

When autumn comes, the beavers start to fill their larder for the winter. They collect leafy branches and submerge them in the lake, where the near-freezing water will keep them fresh and green. As the temperature drops, the woodland trees lose their leaves, the ground becomes covered with snow, and the lake ices over. However, the beavers are well prepared. The roof of their lodge freezes solid, making it practically impenetrable, and their food stores sit safely at the bottom of the lake.

However, the beavers are not always as isolated as they might think. Inside the lodge it is always pitch black, and muskrats have been observed taking advantage of this, joining the beavers in their lodge, and sharing their food. The beavers don't respond in any way, and seem to be either oblivious or indifferent to the muskrats' presence.

Which insects are used for cleaning museums?

This sounds like a mistake. Surely you clean museums of insects, not with them? Nonetheless, there is a type of beetle that museum curators find extremely useful. The dermestid beetle eats dead skin, flesh and hair, and one single beetle can strip the skin off a dead animal in just a few hours, leaving a perfect, pristine skeleton. Natural history museums use these amazing nibblers to clean animal bones that are to be used as exhibits. They are also used by taxidermists, for similar purposes.

Dermestid beetles can also be used by the police to help calculate how long a body has been dead, in a science called forensic entomology. Investigators generally focus on flies and maggots, which are usually the first on the scene; but,

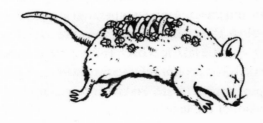

if a body has been left to decay for some time, the presence of beetles is also a useful indicator. Dermestid beetles will appear during the final stages of decomposition, and feed on the dried skin, tendon and bone left behind by the earlier scavengers. Dermestids usually appear around five to eleven days after death.

As well as preying on the dead, dermestids also have a tendency to annoy the living. They are omnivores, who love to eat grain, and they cause millions of dollars' worth of crop damage every year, making them a major irritation for farmers. They can also cause havoc in your home, if you're unlucky enough to become infested. Let a dermestid beetle into your home, and it will munch your carpet right down to the bare floorboards.

Which reptile solves crime?

No, it's not the premise for a new Pixar film. There really is a type of reptile that has helped the police solve crimes. Snapping turtles are freshwater turtles that are found in the Americas. There are two species: the enormous alligator snapping turtle, which can weigh as much as 100 kilograms (about 16 stone); and the common snapping turtle, which is smaller, rarely weighing more than 30 kilograms (around 5 stone). Both species have a large head, which they cannot withdraw into their small shell. They have very strong jaws, and mobile necks, and will bite aggressively if threatened.

Snapping turtles like to eat rotting meat, and they have a particular talent for sniffing out dead carcasses in the water. This ability has led police to use snapping turtles to help them find human corpses underwater. According to reports, the police simply tie a line to the turtle, and it leads them straight to the body.

They have also been used in a rather ghoulish plan to clean up the River Ganges in India. The river is traditionally a holy site, into which people cast the corpses of their loved ones, in the belief that the sacred river will purify the soul of the deceased. Thanks to this practice, as well as the by-products of local industry and agriculture, the river is horribly polluted. In one attempt to clean it, the authorities introduced thousands of snapping turtles into the river, having first trained them to feed only on dead flesh, to prevent them from attacking swimmers, as can be their wont. However, it's not clear how successful the plan has been, since dead bodies are still frequently seen floating on the holy waters.

Do birds have accents?

A bird's ability to sing is partly inherited, and partly taught by its parents. Scientists have demonstrated this by conducting tests on chaffinch chicks. If the chicks are reared in silence, they will still attempt to sing, but their calls will be only barely recognisable as chaffinch calls. They have to hear their parents sing before they are able to produce the full range and subtleties of the usual chaffinch song.

Since these songs are passed down through the generations, we might therefore imagine that birds in different regions would develop distinctive, regional accents. And this turns out to be true. Experts can recognise the different accents of chaffinches from the north of England compared with those from the south.

In the nineteenth century, Australian settlers imported many plant and animal species from Europe, to help themselves feel more at home in this strange new land. These included a range of songbirds, such as blackbirds, which were not indigenous to Australia. Today, little more than a century later, the descendants of those blackbirds have developed a distinctive Australian accent.

What is a remote-control cockroach?

Cockroaches may be unpleasant, but they are also remarkable creatures, and we can learn a great deal from them. Scientists love cockroaches, because they're great for experimenting on. The nerve cells in their brains are quite similar to ours, and they also grow tumours that are like those of humans. As a result, scientists use cockroaches to study cancer, heart disease, and even the inner workings of the brain.

In one fascinating experiment, scientists at the University of Tokyo found that they could remove a cockroach's wings, insert tiny electrodes into its antennae, and use these to 'drive' it via remote control, making it stop, go, and turn left and right. To power the electrodes, the cockroaches were also fitted with tiny backpacks, containing a battery.

Now this experiment may sound frivolous, but it could

have valuable applications. Scientists are looking into the possibility of using remote-control cockroaches in rescue work. With tiny cameras on their backs, cockroaches could be incredibly useful in exploring collapsed buildings and other dangerous, inaccessible locations.

In fact, cockroaches are not the only creatures to have been experimented on in this way. In recent years, scientists have carried out similar tests on remote-control rats, pigeons and sharks. In theory, remote-control animals like these could have numerous useful applications, such as military surveillance, clearing landmines or mapping underground areas. The advantage of using real animals in this way, rather than building robots, is that these animals can already deal with problems such as walking, turning, climbing and avoiding obstacles, which turn out to actually be very difficult for real robots to accomplish, at least at present.

How do cuttlefish change colour?

The cuttlefish surely has the most astonishing talent for camouflage of any creature. Let's compare it to its nearest competitor: the chameleon. A chameleon can change its colour completely in about ten to fifteen seconds, by moving layers of coloured pigment inside its skin cells.

Using just a handful of basic pigment colours, it is able to produce a wide range of colours. This ability is certainly impressive.

However, cuttlefish have millions of these pigment cells, and they can turn them on or off as quickly as we can blink. This means that cuttlefish can change colour hundreds of times per second. They can also produce dazzling effects, such as making colours move in rippling waves along their bodies.

However, perhaps the most intriguing aspect of the cuttlefish's ability is that it can camouflage itself incredibly quickly, instantly matching the hues and shades of the rocks and seaweed around it, despite being completely colour blind. Scientists believe that cuttlefish can respond to differences in the contrast of their environment of as little as 15 per cent, and can even match their body patterns to objects nearby. But as for how they do it, while seemingly being unable to see the colours they are mimicking, we simply don't know.

Can dogs smell cancer?

Dogs have an extraordinary sense of smell. A human nose contains about 5 million olfactory cells, whereas a dog's has 220 million. A dog's sense of smell is not only hundreds of times better than ours, it is also four times better than the best odour-detecting machines we can build. This amazing skill makes dogs extremely useful for human purposes, as we can train them to sniff out guns, drugs, explosives, dead bodies; in fact, they can be trained to sniff out almost anything.

Amazingly, they can even detect cancer. In tests, doctors in California found that Labradors and Portuguese water dogs could detect lung and breast cancer more accurately than any high-tech screening equipment such as mammograms or CT scans. Simply by smelling the patient's breath, the dogs correctly identified 99 per cent of patients suffering from lung cancer, and 88 per cent of breast cancer sufferers. They maintained this high level of accuracy even when the results were adjusted to take into account whether the lung cancer patients were smokers. Studies have also indicated that dogs are able to detect melanomas and bladder cancers.

This may even lead to dogs one day being actively used in patient care or diagnosis. Alternatively, scientists may be able to identify exactly which gas compounds the dogs are reacting to, and use this knowledge to develop more accurate screening technology. One possibility that is currently being developed is a breathalyser to detect lung cancer.

Who was the last known speaker of Ature?

Ature was the language of the Atures people of Venezuela, but the language died out during the nineteenth century. The German explorer and geographer Alexander von Humboldt was lucky enough to meet the very last speaker of this language, while trekking through the Venezuelan jungle.

During his expedition, von Humboldt had made many fascinating discoveries, including the electric eel, the Brazil nut and a previously undiscovered ocean current off the west coast of South America. However, he had not managed to discover a single word of the Ature language.

Then, while visiting the neighbouring tribe of Maypures, he finally made a breakthrough. He was led by torchlight through the remote village, to the cage of a talking parrot. The Maypures explained that this bird had been captured long ago, from the Atures people, who were now extinct. The bird began to speak, reciting its limited vocabulary, which comprised the only extant record of what had once been an entire language.

Nonetheless, von Humboldt recorded the forty words that the parrot knew, and so we do still at least have those. In 1997, artist Rachel Berwick taught these words to a group of parrots, with the help of a linguist and a parrot expert. She then exhibited the talking birds as an artwork, in a cylindrical aviary made of translucent plastic.

Which amphibian can survive being frozen?

Alaska and Canada are home to several hardy frog species, which somehow have to survive the icy winter. The solution found by two of them, wood frogs and chorus frogs, is that their bodies can be frozen almost solid, and still survive. In this state of hibernation, more than two-thirds of the water in the frogs' bodies turns to ice, and their hearts stop. If you were to pick one up and cut it with a knife, it wouldn't bleed. Nonetheless, it is still alive.

In most animals, freezing temperatures are dangerous because they cause ice crystals to form, which can rupture the soft walls of blood vessels. Freezing can also damage skin and blood cells, which is what we mean when we refer to frostbite. However, these amazing frogs have found a way of surviving these threats. When ice starts to form on their bodies, they begin producing extra glucose in their livers, and this functions as antifreeze, flowing into their body's cells and preventing them from being damaged through freezing. Simultaneously, water drains out of the cells and into the spaces between them. This water will freeze, but it will not harm the body's organs. Having survived the winter, the frogs will then begin to thaw as the temperature rises in spring.

There are a number of other creatures that can survive sub-zero temperatures. The Arctic woolly bear caterpillar can survive being frozen solid for ten months in the tundra, where temperatures drop below minus 50 degrees Celsius, with no ill effects. The Arctic ground squirrel also allows its body temperature to drop below freezing, and survives.

However, so far scientists haven't found an equivalent antifreeze like that of the wood frogs, so it's still unclear how this squirrel manages to survive the cold.

The Siberian salamander can also survive in temperatures as low as minus 50 degrees Celsius. It too produces a kind of antifreeze chemical before it hibernates, which protects its cells from rupturing. A story even arose that salamanders could stay frozen for centuries, after researchers found a frozen salamander beside the body of a mammoth excavated from the permafrost, which then came back to life when it thawed out. However, it now seems that the salamander had not frozen at the same time as the woolly mammoth, but rather had slipped down a crack during the previous season.

Scorpions are normally found only in warm countries, but nonetheless their tolerance to a range of different climactic conditions is amazing. Scorpions can withstand freezing for several weeks, and can survive being underwater for two days. Their exoskeleton retains liquid so well that they can live in the hottest deserts. Their appetite is so small that individuals of some species can go without any food or water for an astonishing twelve months. To top it all, some scorpions can live for as long as thirty years.

How do gas companies employ vultures?

For centuries, people have wondered how vultures, circling high in the sky, are able to detect corpses lying on the grasslands. Do they have an extremely acute sense of sight? Or, on the other hand, can they smell the corpse? This question led to an extremely bitter debate during the nineteenth century between the English naturalist Charles Waterton, who insisted that turkey vultures were attracted to carrion by smell, and the American ornithologist John James Audubon, who was equally adamant that vultures found their meals by sight. Both camps had their supporters, but, without any convincing evidence either way, the debate managed to continue for decades without resolution.

It never seemed to occur to anyone that different species of vulture might function in different ways. As we now know, African and American vultures are not closely related, despite their apparent similarities, so there is no reason to assume that they would both find their food in the same way. In fact, we now know that African vultures find their meals purely by sight, whereas many species of American vulture also have a keen sense of smell.

In the 1930s, new evidence appeared, which helped to advance the debate. Gas companies in California were struggling to locate the various leaks that cropped up in a 48-kilometre (30-mile) stretch of pipeline that carried gas across rough terrain. A solution was found when someone noticed that turkey vultures seemed to be attracted to the site of gas leaks. The birds were seemingly attracted by the smell of gas, or rather the smell of mercaptan, the substance which gas companies put into commercial gas supplies, which are otherwise odourless, and therefore potentially dangerous. To test this, the gas companies increased the amount of mercaptan in their gas, and saw that vultures would indeed congregate above the site of any leak, showing engineers exactly where the pipeline needed repairing. The reason for this is that ethyl mercaptan is a gas produced by dead animals during the first stages of decay. It is this gas that attracts the turkey vultures, demonstrating that they are attracted to carrion by their sense of smell.

Can sharks really tie knots?

Sharks are one of the most difficult creatures for scientists to observe. In captivity, their behaviour is usually muted or otherwise altered by the cramped conditions, predictable feeding patterns, and human interaction. In the wild, little meaningful behaviour can be seen from the surface, and in the deep, where sharks tend to operate, it's too dark to see them, even if they were to allow us to get close enough to do so, which they don't.

As a result, there is a great deal that we don't know. One of the most fascinating mysteries concerns how sharks give birth. When sharks mate, the male fertilises the female's egg by inserting one of his claspers into her cloaca. (A cloaca is a cavity at the end of the digestive tract. A clasper is a fingerlike appendage, a bit like a penis, which the male uses to inseminate the female. And, yes, we did say 'claspers', plural, because he has two!) In many species of shark, the egg then grows inside the female for many months, until she eventually gives birth to fully formed shark pups, which are immediately capable of fending for themselves.

However, in some species, the female lays an egg-filled sac, known as a mermaid's purse, at the bottom of the ocean. Some sharks even attach the egg sacs to coral, tying the sacs on with what looks like a kind of yellow string, using an intricate knot. Deep-sea divers who have seen mermaid's purses describe them as being transparent, silver pouches. Apparently, you can even see the baby sharks wriggling inside. But how on earth can a shark tie a knot? For now, we simply don't know.

Which bird can sew?

There are a number of species of bird that have developed sewing skills, which they use to construct their nests. Examples include three birds of the warbler family: the golden-headed cisticola in Australia, the evergreen forest warbler in Africa and the suitably named tailor bird of India. Each of these birds has a long, thin beak, which it uses like a needle. For thread, they use spiders' silk, cotton from seeds, and fibres from the bark of trees.

To sew, the bird selects two leaves that are still growing and attached, and holds their edges together. Then, holding a fibre in its beak, it makes a hole in both leaves, and threads the fibre through. It twists both ends of this thread, locking the stitch in place. It takes about six of these stitches to turn a pair of leaves into a cup, which can then be filled with grass, and used as a nest.

There are other birds that practise an even more difficult craft: weaving. In South America, orioles, oropendolas and caciques all weave their nests. In Africa, there are a number of sparrow species that weave. They do so by tearing a fibrous strip from a leaf, and threading it alternately over and under other strips. This is a difficult business, as it requires some degree of forward planning and judgement, since the bird has to decide how taut each strip should be, how much each wall of the planned structure should curve, and what the final shape should be. Some of the nests built in this way are extremely neat and precise.

Other woven nests are impressive for different reasons. The nest of the sociable weaver, which is found in south-western Africa, could not be called neat. In truth, it barely deserves to be described as 'weaving' at all, because the nest is constructed by simply piling stems of dried grass on top of one another, between the branches of a tree. However, what they lack in beauty, they make up for in size. These nests are immense, forming giant apartment blocks that serve as the year-round home for as many as a hundred families. They are also incredibly durable – some are thought to be more than a century old.

The birds live in tunnels, which open at the bottom of the stack. Some of these tunnels lead up into nesting chambers, while others are dead ends, in which the birds roost. The top of the stack consists of a thatched roof, which is made using thicker grass stems, and which all the birds maintain. These nests are ideally suited to the hot desert environment. In the day, they shelter the birds from the heat of the sun; at night, the nest chambers retain much of their heat, while outside the temperature drops below freezing.

How do catfish predict earthquakes?

Catfish have the most finely tuned senses of any creature. They have more taste buds than any other animals – in fact, their entire bodies are covered in them. Their senses of smell, hearing and touch are also amazingly powerful. Catfish can smell some compounds at a dilution of just one part in 10 billion.

They can also pick up ultra-low-frequency sound using their 'lateral line', which is a line of small pores along the fish's side. These pores contain tiny hairlike projections that are incredibly sensitive to vibrations. For centuries, Chinese people have taken advantage of the catfish's amazing abilities, using the fish to warn of earthquakes. People say that the fish can sense when an earthquake is coming days in advance.

There is also evidence that some other animals can sense earthquakes. After the Indian Ocean tsunami in December 2004, there were numerous reports of strange animal behaviour. At the Yala National Park in Sri Lanka, where sixty humans died, not one animal was killed. On India's Cuddalore coast, where thousands of people died, the local goats, buffalo and other animals seemed to have escaped largely unharmed. There were various anecdotal reports of animals running for higher ground, and abandoning their usual territories, in the days leading up to the tsunami.

This raises the question of how the animals would have sensed that an earthquake was coming. One possible explanation is that the animals may have sensed the electromagnetic disturbances that accompanied the fracturing of rocks before the earthquake. In, 1998 scientists in Japan tested this ability by observing laboratory animals' behaviour while blocks of granite were mechanically crushed nearby. As the pressure on the blocks grew, the animals visibly became more anxious, which seemed to be linked to the emergence of electromagnetic effects from the rocks.

Which spider builds its home underwater?

There is an amazing spider that is able to spend its life underwater even though, like all spiders, it cannot breathe in water. So how does it do it? The answer is that it builds itself an airtight underwater capsule, which it fills with oxygen, and lives inside. It is, appropriately enough, known as the water spider, or diving bell spider.

The first stage is to weave a tight web underwater, between two plant stems. The spider manages to stay submerged by breathing the bubbles of air that get trapped in the hairs of its abdomen, and it frequently returns to the surface. Once the web is complete, the spider surfaces once more, before diving back in, taking with it a large bubble of air captured between its two hind legs. It swims with its other six legs, which is hard work, since the bubble of air is buoyant, and spiders' long, thin legs are not designed for swimming. Nonetheless, the spider eventually makes it down to the web, under which it traps the bubble of air, as well as any other bubbles trapped in its abdomen. It repeats this step many more times, frequently adding more threads to support and expand the web, until this underwater air chamber is about the size of an acorn, making it considerably bigger than the spider, which is just 12 millimetres (half an inch) long.

From this chamber, the spider hunts, darting out at unsuspecting prey, which may include passing tadpoles, small fish and other pond life. Sometimes, it eats insects that have been unlucky enough to fall in the water. It swims to the surface to grab them, and then drags them back to its chamber.

Like all spiders, the water spider feeds by breaking down its food using digestive fluids from its salivary glands, which means it needs to return to its bubble to eat, because it can't carry out this process in water. A further difficulty is that the oxygen in the spider's bubble does eventually run out, but when it needs more, the spider simply swims to the surface, and brings down another bubble. Amazingly, the spider doesn't just hunt underwater. It lives in this diving bell, even mating here, and bringing up its young!

What is an aphid farm?

Aphids are small insects that feed predominantly on the sugary sap of plants. This sap is full of energy, but short on nitrogen, which is an essential part of the aphids' diet, so they need to drink a great deal of sap. They get rid of the sugary excess either by excreting it or allowing it to grow out of their bodies, in a big, sugary drop of honeydew. Honeydew may be a waste product for aphids, but ants prize it very highly.

When ants find a large group of aphids, they will milk them for their honeydew, like farmers milking cattle. It is an appropriate analogy, as the ants will tend and protect a herd of aphids in much the same way as a farmer looks after his cattle. Ants will build a shelter of leaves and soil to shield the aphids from rain, or fence them in. They herd the aphids back to the ant colony at night, and may then take them to a new spot to graze the next day, even selecting plants that will lead to higher production of honeydew. The ants' effort is well rewarded, because the aphids can produce more than their own weight in honeydew in a single hour. Some aphid species even produce three times as much honeydew if regularly milked, just like cattle.

The ants can even interfere with the aphids' natural cycle. Under normal circumstances, when a population of aphids reaches a given size, some of them will turn into sexually mature winged forms, and fly away to mate. However, this wouldn't suit the ant farmers, and so they produce a hormone that delays the aphids' sexual maturity, allowing the herd to grow to an unnatural, but productive, size.

Ants are not just cattle farmers. There are also more than 200 species of ants that are arable farmers, growing fungi for food. Leaf-cutter ants do not eat the leaves they collect – instead, they grow fungus gardens on the leaves, and eat the fungi. These ants tend their gardens carefully, keeping them well fertilised, and free of bacteria, pests and mould. Amazingly, the fungi that these ants grow are found nowhere else on earth.

However, sometimes fungi can turn the tables, and farm ants. There is a fungus called *Cordyceps*, whose spores can find their way into the body of the South American bullet ant. If this occurs, the fungus releases a pheromone that scrambles the ant's usual behaviours. The confused ant will climb to the top of a tall plant stem, and lock itself in place with its jaws. Once the ant is in place, the fungus's fruiting body erupts as a spike from the insect's brain, sprinkling a fine dust of spores over the ants working below.

What is 'civet'?

Civets are mammals found in the tropical regions of Africa and Asia. They look like a cross between a cat and a mongoose, with dark, mottled fur. Civets are tree dwellers, whose diet consists of fruit, insects, worms, and some small vertebrates such as squirrels, rats and birds.

However, 'civet' is also the name given to the musk produced by the civet's perineal gland, which is found just next to its anus. Civets smear this oil on their dunghills, as well as on rocks and branches in their territory, as a sign of ownership, to warn off rivals. 'Civet', in this sense, is a thick, oily substance, with such a powerful, unpleasant smell that the tiniest whiff of it can actually make a person physically sick. Many other small mammals, including cats, badgers, skunks and weasels, have similar anal secretions, which they use to mark their territory.

Given their purpose, it makes sense that these secretions would have evolved to become extremely potent and long-lasting. This combination of potency and endurance has meant that civet oil has become highly prized by perfumers, the people who make perfumes. Although it smells terrible on its own, civet oil has an amazing effect when combined with other scents: it 'exalts' them, meaning that it heightens their smell, making them come to life, and giving them weight and depth. It also makes them release their scent extremely slowly, so that the perfume retains its power for a long time.

Manufacturers of perfumes are not required to reveal the ingredients used in their products, so the compositions of most fine fragrances remain a well-guarded secret. However, until fairly recently, civet oil is thought to have been widely used in many popular perfumes, with luxury brands such as Chanel, Lancome, and Cartier all admitting to using it in their products. Even the world's most celebrated perfume, Chanel No. 5, was found in laboratory tests to contain civet, although Chanel claim that, since 1998, they have used synthetic civet oil rather than the real thing.

One reason for the increasing use of synthetic civet oil, rather than the real thing, is that today consumers and manufacturers are more aware of the cruelty involved in the practice of collecting real civet. In the past, civets were frequently hunted and killed for their musk. Today, they are more likely to be kept alive, in tiny cages, with the musk regularly harvested by scraping it from their perineal gland, in what is surely a painful and unpleasant procedure.

Can a frog tell you whether or not you are pregnant?

Amazingly, before the 1960s, the best available pregnancy test was to inject a woman's urine into the back of a frog. Doctors would inject the urine into the frog's dorsal lymph sac in the morning, and then check back at the end of the day. If the woman was pregnant, a dose of her urine would cause the female frog to lay eggs within twelve hours. This test also works on male frogs, albeit in a different way – in that case, if the woman is pregnant, her urine will cause male frogs to produce sperm.

The test works because the urine of a pregnant woman contains a hormone called human chorionic gonadotropin, or hCG. It is this hormone that modern home pregnancy kits test for, but they do so using prepared antibodies. However, these tests were made possible only by the development in 1959 of a new sensitive technique for measuring antigens. Before this discovery, the frog test was the best of a very limited range of options.

The first test of this kind was developed in the 1920s by chemist Selmar Aschheim and gynaecologist Bernhard Zondek. In this procedure, which was known as the 'A–Z test', the doctors would inject five female mice with a woman's urine several times over the course of a number of days. They would then dissect the mice, and examine their ovaries. If the ovaries were enlarged, this would indicate that the woman was pregnant. Within a few years, a similar test was developed using rabbits.

In 1930, a British zoologist based in South Africa, called Lancelot Hogben, found a way to control ovulation in the South African clawed frog, by using ox hormones. Frogs normally ovulate only during the spawning season, which had previously meant that they were unsuitable for use in pregnancy testing, which of course needs to take place all year round. However, if this problem were to be overcome, frogs would be ideal for testing. Frogs produce large eggs, which are kept outside of the body, meaning that it would not be necessary to kill the frogs to observe the results, and so they could be reused, unlike mice or rabbits. Thanks to Hogben's discovery, by 1933 doctors were using the clawed frog to test for hCG, and, over the following two decades, it was the most reliable and preferred method of testing for pregnancy.

However, one problem with the Hogben test was that it created a huge demand for South African clawed frogs, which were native only to southern Africa. Scientists elsewhere could farm them in captivity, but it tended to be easier to import them in large numbers. Even so, testing centres could quickly become overrun by disease, and so when simpler, chemical tests were developed in the 1960s, the Hogben test became obsolete.

Scientists now believe that the use of frogs in pregnancy tests may have inadvertently led to the extinction of dozens of species of amphibians. The South African clawed frog is resistant to an amphibian fungus called *Batrachochytrium dendrobatidis*, but it can carry it, and transmit it to other frog species. This fungus is thought to have originated in Africa, and then been transmitted by the clawed frog, when it was exported to all parts of the world. Infection causes frogs to shed an excessive amount of skin, and exhibit strange behaviours, such as nocturnal frogs coming out into the open during the daytime. Scientists think this fungus may be responsible for a large number of amphibian extinctions, including two-thirds of the 110 species of harlequin frogs from South and Central America.

CHAPTER TWO

Peculiar parents

Which amphibian feeds her own skin to her young?

Caecilians look like worms, and live in the ground, but they are actually amphibians. They are found in the tropical regions of Asia, Africa and South America, and there are at least 170 species of them, and probably many more. One of these species, *Boulengerula taitanus*, has an extraordinary way of feeding her young. When she has laid her cluster of eggs, she then curls her long body around them protectively. Once they hatch, the young start to bite her flanks, tearing off strips of her skin. She allows this to happen, until they have eaten the entire outer layer of her body. This takes place in a frenzy, which lasts about seven minutes. The family will then rest for three days, giving the mother time to grow a new layer of skin, before they tuck in again.

You might think that this would hurt or damage the mother, but actually it seems to do her no harm. This is because she grows a new, outer layer of skin, making her twice as thick as before, for just this purpose. Like mammals' milk, the caecilian's new skin contains high levels of lipids, making it an excellent source of nutrients for the growing larvae. This practice is known as dermatotrophy, and is highly unusual. The caecilian is the only amphibian known to practise it.

There is another species of caecilian that has a similarly bizarre way of feeding her young. In this species, the mother retains her eggs within her oviduct – the tube through which the egg passes – for much longer, so that the larvae hatch while still inside her. These larvae also feast on the mother's body tissues, but, rather than gnawing on her external skin, instead they eat the interior lining of her oviduct. In this species, the larvae can remain within their mother, cannibalising her in this bizarre way, for up to eleven months.

After giving birth, why do many mammals eat the afterbirth?

There seems to be no definitive answer, but there are a number of compelling theories. Some believe that the placenta is full of nutrients, which a new mother desperately needs to recover from the ordeal of childbirth, and to support the production of milk to feed her young. Some mammals avoid all food during the last twenty-four hours of pregnancy, which may be another reason why they desperately crave nutrition at this point.

Another commonly held theory is that animals eat the placenta to hide evidence of childbirth from predators in the wild. However, there are a number of problems with this theory. Many dominant, unchallenged predatory species also eat their afterbirth, even though they face no obvious threats. Some tree-dwelling primates, which even give birth up a tree, will then spend an hour or two eating the afterbirth, when they could safely drop it to the ground. Furthermore, placenta-eating mammals don't clean up the amniotic fluid produced during childbirth, which one would think might also attract predators, if this was the concern.

A more likely explanation seems to be that the placenta contains a number of useful chemicals. It contains high levels of the hormone prostaglandin, which helps the uterus to return to its former shape. It also contains the hormone oxytocin, which stimulates the production of breast milk. The placenta is also believed to contain a painkiller called placental opioid-enhancing factor. There is also a belief that, among humans, eating the placenta helps to prevent postpartum depression, although there seems to be no scientific basis for this.

The societies of many Pacific islands have a rather more pleasant tradition. Rather than eating the placenta, mothers will often take it home, bury it in the garden (or, one hopes, have it buried for them), then plant a tree over it, which will grow and flourish over the lifetime of the child.

Which bird incubates its eggs on a pile of rotting compost?

Megapodes are a group of chicken-sized birds that are found in the Pacific Islands near Australia and Indonesia. They are browsers, who spend their lives on the ground, kicking through the leaf litter in search of seeds, fruit, snails and worms. When it's time to breed, a group of the birds, males and females, will start to kick the leaf litter into a pile, which soon becomes a mound, and eventually a huge mound, perhaps 4.5 metres (15 feet) high and 10 metres (33 feet) across.

The mound contains a lot of vegetable matter, which slowly rots, heating the temperature inside the mound as it does so. The females now dig burrows in the mound, into which they lay their eggs, a few feet below the surface, one to a burrow. Then, each burrow is filled in, and the megapodes leave the mound. The reason they can leave their eggs unattended is that the temperature inside the mound is remarkably stable; at the depth where the eggs are placed, it remains at 35–39 degrees Celsius (95–102 degrees Fahrenheit). Around six to nine weeks later, the eggs will hatch, and the chicks will climb their way to the surface. Within twenty-four hours, they can fly.

Why do some parents kill their own young?

We like to think of animals nurturing and caring for their young. As well as appealing to our sense of morality, it also just seems to make sense. Most animals try to have as many offspring as they can, and to give them the best possible chance in life, to ensure that their genes are passed on. So how on earth could a species have evolved a tendency or desire to kill their own young?

Well, any species in which the parents routinely killed their young would surely be doomed to a rapid extinction, but the possibility of occasionally killing some of your brood might have evolved as a by-product of some behaviour that was otherwise beneficial. For example, many mammal mothers lick the wounds of their young, including dogs, cats, and primates, and in most cases this is a useful and therapeutic act. The licking action cleans the wound, and the mother's saliva usually has some antibacterial property to lessen the risk of infection. However, in some cases where the offspring shows no improvement, the mother may persist in licking it, and go on to eat the baby. In some cases, she may then go on to eat all her offspring, including those that are perfectly healthy.

Other examples of animals that kill their own young

are perhaps harder to explain. In a number of mammal species, mothers will sometimes appear to deliberately kill their newborn offspring. This occurs fairly frequently among pigs, frequently enough for it have a specific term: savaging. It is estimated that around 5 per cent of first-time pig mothers, or gilts, will kill at least one of their litter. This rate can be reduced if the gilts are kept near to experienced sows. This kind of maternal infanticide has also been observed in rabbits and beetles.

Some fathers are also known to kill their own offspring. When young bass fish hatch, the father plays a protective role, guarding the area around them, and circling the group to keep them together. However, after a few days most of the young fish will swim away, and from this point on the father treats any stragglers as if they were any other small fish, which is to say that he eats them. Presumably, after a certain time, he no longer recognises them as his own.

How do eels reproduce?

Eels are one of the world's most mysterious creatures. We have never been able to observe their reproductive habits, and so much of what we believe about how they breed is based on inference and assumption. Aristotle carried out the first known research on eels. He believed that they simply grew from the earth, 'from the guts of wet soil'. For centuries, no one was able to contradict this theory, because no one ever saw any evidence that actively disproved it.

It is now believed that all European eels are born as saltwater fish in the Sargasso Sea, an eerily calm area of the North Atlantic that is full of sargassum weed. These fish, which are effectively the eel larvae, then travel about 4,800 kilometres (3,000 miles) on the Gulf Stream, where they enter the mouth of whichever European river they arrive at first. As they make their journey into the conti-nent, they can overcome tremendous challenges. They can travel through wet grass, or wet sand, and climb enormous obstacles en masse, by making piles of their bodies tens of thousands high. Once they reach freshwater, they trans-form into freshwater eels, or 'elvers', and begin to feed on insects, worms and small crustaceans.

They remain living as elvers for many years until they eventually reach sexual maturity, which occurs at anywhere between six and forty years, depending upon the species. When this happens, the eel transforms itself once again, seemingly in preparation for the long journey back to the Sargasso Sea. It becomes tougher and heavier, storing fat for the journey. Its belly turns silver and its back becomes darker, perhaps to camouflage it from ocean predators. The eel's head becomes pointed, its eyes swell up, and its nostrils dilate. The salt content in its body decreases, and its sex organs become bigger. Also, the eel's gas bladder changes, allowing it to endure pressures of one ton per square inch.

Once the eels reach the Sargasso, it is believed that the females spawn, the males fertilise the eggs, and then they both die of exhaustion. However, no one has ever seen an eel spawn in the Sargasso, or an adult die of exhaustion there. No one has ever seen an eel egg, and no eels have ever been bred in captivity. For some reason, when scientists capture an eel, its reproductive system shuts down immediately, as if refusing to share its secrets.

Why do birds of prey encourage their young to kill one another?

As unpleasant as it may sound, many birds of prey, such as the harpy eagle and the bald eagle, will usually lay two eggs, and then encourage one of the hatchlings to kill and eat the other. The parents will usually give the elder sibling most of the food, and allow it to bully and harass the younger one until it dies. The first-born now eats his younger sibling, which means that the energy and nutrition that the parents invested in the second hatchling all gets usefully reinvested. The reason for this shocking approach to parenting seems to be that the birds' best chance of raising healthy offspring is to focus all their resources and energy on one chick, and so the second egg is little more than an insurance policy, in case the first egg is infertile, or gets destroyed in some way.

The macaroni penguin does something slightly different. It also lays two eggs, but the first egg it lays is notably disadvantaged compared with the second. It is less than two-thirds the size of the second egg, it hatches later, and consequently it rarely survives. The reason the first egg is so frail seems to be that the penguins' eggs are in most danger of getting eaten or destroyed at the start of the breeding season, when the colony is just getting established. During this time, the adults are busy fighting, and skuas steal many of the eggs. Therefore, the penguins have evolved a tendency to favour the second egg, which is more likely to result in a healthy offspring.

Another species of bird has even evolved a special weapon, which is present only in the hatchlings, and seems to exist purely for the purpose of killing the bird's own siblings. Asian blue-throated bee-eaters lay large clutches of eggs, hatching as many as seventeen baby birds. Each of them has a sharp hook on the tip of its beak, which it uses to slash at its brothers and sisters inside the darkness of the nest hole. Over the next two weeks, most of them will die from these injuries, while the strongest candidates will grow feathers, which protect them from the hooks. The survivors' own hooks will by now have been worn away, and so the remaining birds will now live together more harmoniously.

Which bird is a real homewrecker?

The house sparrow is native to Europe, Asia and parts of North Africa, but it has been successfully introduced in every temperate part of the world, making it the world's most widely distributed wild bird. It was introduced to North America in 1851, when a hundred birds were released in Brooklyn, New York. By 1900, the population had spread as far west as the Rocky Mountains. One possible reason for the bird's success in populating new territories is its aggressive nature. One scientist in 1889 reported instances of house sparrows attacking seventy other bird species. They also often evict other birds from their nests; frequent victims are house martins, bluebirds and sand martins. House sparrows will sometimes even build a new nest right on top of another bird's active nest, even while there are live young still nesting there.

House sparrows are also homewreckers in another sense, as their romantic lives are remarkably dramatic. Both males and females take multiple partners, and house sparrows have one of the shortest incubation periods of all birds, just ten to twelve days, producing clutches of five or six eggs. When a male finds a female, he will often destroy all her eggs, and kill any chicks, which bizarrely is his way of persuading her to mate with him. Females whose eggs have hatched will devote most of their energy to incubating and caring for their young, so destroying them makes the female once again available to breed.

In cases where the male house sparrow has a number of 'wives', the second wife will sometimes seek out and destroy the nest of the first wife, killing all her chicks. This seems to be her only way of getting the male to help raise her chicks, since otherwise he would feed only the chicks of his first wife. Only if the second wife kills this first brood will the male then help to feed and raise his second family. Thus, killing the rival chicks simply ensures that her own chicks get the best care possible.

Which creature kills its siblings while still in the womb?

The sand tiger shark is a fierce-looking predator, which is found in coastal waters all over the world. Despite its appearance and considerable size – it can grow to a length of more than 3 metres (10 feet) – it is not regarded as being particularly aggressive, although there have been some reported attacks on humans, some of which have been fatal.

This shark has a fascinating and gruesome way of reproducing. It has two wombs, which each contain a number of fertilised eggs. When all the yolk has been eaten, the baby sharks will hatch, while still inside their mother's womb. Now, the first ones to hatch will quickly seek out and eat all the unhatched eggs. They then start to hunt down and kill one another, until there remain just two survivors, one in each womb.

It's usually the case that the first shark to hatch in each womb will be the one to survive, as it will have had a significant head start on its siblings. One advantage of having two wombs is that the shark will usually end up producing two healthy, well-fed offspring. To provide further nourishment, the mother will continue to produce eggs for the two survivors to eat.

They remain inside their mother for an astonishing two years, until they reach around a metre (just over 3 feet) long, and are quite capable of fending for themselves. This is important, because, as soon as they are born, they will have to hunt and feed and defend themselves independently. Amazingly, there are reports of scientists touching the bellies of heavily pregnant sand tiger sharks, and having their fingers nipped by the sharp, fully developed teeth of the young sharks, still inside the womb!

Why are coot parents so cruel?

European coot parents treat their young with extreme discipline. If one of the chicks becomes greedy or pushy, or squawks too loudly, its parents will pick it up and rebuke it by shaking it furiously. They may even duck it in the water, leaving the poor chick so traumatised by the experience that it may hide in the reeds while the parents feed the other siblings. Sometimes, the distressed chick will never return to the nest. This kind of strict discipline means that the broods of European coots quickly diminish from seven down to three.

American coots belong to a separate species, and their behaviour is also somewhat different. When American coot chicks beg for food, they display their exotic plumage. The chicks have a bright tuft of orange down on their heads, along with a bright-red bald patch. The parents will feed the chicks with the brightest colours first, because these are likely to be the strongest and healthiest, and thus the ones most likely to survive. As a result of this preferential feeding, the broods of American coots also diminish quickly in size. Each year, around a third of the chicks that hatch die of starvation.

Which amphibian emerges from its mother's back?

The Surinam toad is found in tropical South America, and is a pretty weird creature, even for a toad. It is usually about 10–12 centimetres (4–5 inches) long, and its body is extremely flat, as if it has been trodden on. When two of these toads pair up, they dance together in the water, somersaulting gracefully around one another. The female ejects her eggs, and the male simultaneously releases his sperm, so that the eggs are immediately fertilised in the water. He then spreads the toes of one foot, and, using this foot like a plasterer's trowel, he collects the eggs and spreads them over the female's back. The pair continue to dance together, and each time they somersault, he spreads more eggs onto her back. Gradually, the skin of the female's back starts to swell up, trapping the eggs inside. Within a day or so, the skin will have regrown over the eggs, forming a strange-looking honeycomb.

The eggs now remain trapped within the female's skin, even while they hatch into tadpoles. All the while, they are absorbing nutrients from their mother, and continuing to grow. Soon, you can actually see the tadpoles wriggling underneath her skin. Twenty-four days after fertilisation, they break through the skin of their mother's back, and swim off on their own, not as tadpoles, but as fully developed miniature toads, each less than an inch long.

What is the sad fate of squirrel matrons?

Belding's ground squirrels live in colonies several hundred strong in North America's Sierra Nevada. To guard the colony from predators, they use an early warning sentinel system, similar to that used by numerous birds, insects and primates. Some adults are always on guard, sitting upright, watching the horizon for potential danger. The ground squirrel's predators include eagles, coyotes, weasels and badgers. If the sentry sees a threat, it will give a loud alarm call, sending all the nearby squirrels running for cover.

However, sentry duty is a dangerous job, as sentries are much more likely to be killed by predators. Perhaps for this reason, sentry duty is only carried out by certain types of ground squirrel within the colony. Males and the very young rarely do the job. Females who have no young also do it only rarely. Instead, most of the sentinel duty is carried out by one group: the matrons, the mature females who already have young of their own. Among Belding's ground squirrels, it is the matrons who are given the most dangerous job.

Which male toad likes to give his young a leg-up in life?

Male European midwife toads take an active and ingenious role in the reproductive process. The male will usually live near a pond, in a damp hole in the ground. When he is ready to mate, he will make a series of short, peeping calls, in the hope that a female will respond. If a female does come to visit him, he grabs her firmly between his forelegs, while she begins to produce eggs in strings several dozen long. The male now crouches on all fours, and releases sperm onto the eggs, as they rest on the female's thighs. Then, after about fifteen minutes, he lifts his legs and pushes them into the pile of spawn, tying the eggs onto his thighs with the strings. Once he has collected them all, the female leaves, and he now takes care of the eggs.

The male toad now carries the eggs around with him, strapped to his thighs, for a number of weeks. If the weather is dry, he will take the eggs down to the pond for a dip, so that they stay moist. When it is time for the tadpoles to emerge, he instinctively knows, and so goes down to the pond at night, and lowers his hind legs into the water. Over a couple of hours, the tadpoles will free themselves and swim off, leaving their devoted father behind.

Why do Penduline tits hide their eggs?

The relationship between male and female Penduline tits seems to be a fractious and quarrelsome one. Penduline tits are small, pretty birds, which can reach around 11 centimetres (4.3 inches) in length, and are found in most parts of eastern and southern Europe. The male weaves an impressive, baglike nest, which hangs from a tree, usually over water. It is this pendulous nest that gives the birds their name. Once the nest is completed, the male calls to nearby females, hoping to persuade them to mate. They will tour the various local nests, assessing their size and quality. In general, the female will select the biggest nest available. She indicates her choice by landing on the nest, carrying a beakful of wool, which will form the lining.

Once she has moved in, the female takes over the construction work herself. She brings in more lining, and digs an entrance tube pointing downwards. Once she's happy with her new home, she mates with the male, and begins to lay her eggs. However, this is when things start to get really interesting.

Given the chance, both the male and female will leave the nest as soon as the eggs have been laid, so that they can go and start a second family. However, they will only leave if they know that the eggs in this first nest will be looked after – both of them have already invested too much into this brood to just let the eggs die. Therefore, they each try to leave the incubation and raising of the offspring to the other.

They do this using some fairly sophisticated tactics. Usually, a clutch will comprise six eggs. As a result, once a male notices that his partner has laid six eggs, he will leave at the first opportunity, knowing that she will be forced to stay and look after the eggs, allowing him to go off and build another nest and raise another family.

To counter this risk, the female may start to hide her eggs. After laying two of them, she may bring in more nest lining, and put it on top of them. The male doesn't seem to be able to count or remember how many eggs have been laid, so, as long as they are out of sight, he is unaware of them. He will continue to mate with her, while she continues to lay – and hide – the eggs. Eventually, she will have her six eggs, at which point she removes the lining, exposing the eggs, and scarpers. When the unwitting male returns to the nest, he has no choice but to raise his brood single-handed, while the female goes off and finds another partner.

How do birds decide which of their young to feed?

When a parent bird arrives back at its nest, its chicks plead to be fed, opening their beaks as wide as they can, displaying their bright-red gapes, while the parent has to decide which hungry mouth gets the food. But how does it decide?

It seems that the colour of the chick's gape is crucial. Birds are more likely to feed the chicks that have the brightest, reddest gape. There are a number of possible explanations for this. In some birds, such as young linnets, the red colour of the gapes comes from the blood vessels in the throat. If, however, the chick has already been fed, some of its blood will be diverted to its stomach, to digest the food. Therefore, a brighter gape indicates which chick has not yet been fed.

Alternatively, there is a theory that the parent will feed the bird with the brightest gape because this is a good indication of the bird's health. A red gape indicates that the bird has a high proportion of red carotenoid pigments, which indicate that it has a strong immune system. According to this argument, the parents' choice therefore serves to favour the strongest chicks, who are the best bet for continuing the bird's lineage.

Some parasitic birds have evolved to take advantage of this tendency, by giving their own young particularly bright gapes. Cuckoos lay their eggs into the nests of other birds, including dunnocks, meadow pipits, and Eurasian reed warblers. When the cuckoo chicks hatch, these interlopers will try to push the host's own chicks out of the nest, and beg for food from the parent bird, seemingly using their bright-red gapes to win favour.

Amazingly, one type of cuckoo, the Hodgson's hawk-cuckoo, has even evolved gape-coloured patches under its wings, which seem to simulate additional mouths. The strategy seems to work, as the parent birds of the nest it parasitises do place food into the patches, as if they are fooled into thinking they are the mouths of their young.

Which insect drinks the blood of its own young?

There is a kind of ant, recently discovered in Madagascar, that has an unusual and gruesome way of feeding. The Dracula ant, which is a member of the *Adetomyrma* genus, sucks the blood of its own larvae. It cuts holes into the larvae's bodies, and feeds on the blood that oozes out, which is called haemolymph. The larvae do survive being cannibalised in this way, although they are left marked and scarred.

Although this kind of cannibalistic behaviour is un-known in any other ant species, it does seem to be linked to a more common characteristic. In many ant species, the adult ants are unable to eat solid food, and so they use the larvae to regurgitate their food for them. The only differ-ence with Dracula ants is that, instead of eating the larvae's regurgitated food, they tap right into the source!

Dracula ants are also fascinating for another reason, as they may represent an evolutionary missing link between wasps and ants. Ants are believed to have evolved from wasps around 70–100 million years ago, during the time of the dinosaurs. In modern ants, the gaster, which is the back third of the body, is separated from the thorax by one or two narrow constrictions, a bit like a waist. This allows ants to manoeuvre and twist in tight spaces. However, Dracula ants have no such constrictions. Their gaster is directly connected to their thorax, just as it is in wasps. If genetic testing can determine the relationship of Dracula ants to more recently evolved ant species, it could help to explain how some of the amazing, complex behaviours of ant colonies developed.

Why does one type of lizard lay its eggs inside a termite nest?

Reptiles lay delicate, fragile eggs, which are very sensitive to temperature and moisture. In too dry an environment, the egg's shell would allow too much moisture to escape, drying out the contents, and killing the embryo. If the temperature is too hot or cold, the embryo will also die. Consequently, finding the ideal spot to lay the egg is a crucial part of the reptile's reproductive process.

A number of species of monitor lizard have found an ingenious place to lay their eggs: in the centre of a termite nest. Termite nests are one of the natural world's most amazing constructions. They are built in such a way that the temperature and humidity inside the nest remain perfectly constant. There are shafts and chimneys, to create updraughts within the nest, spreading the hot air gen-erated by the termites working in the basement of the nest. The termites manage the humidity carefully, bringing water up from the water table if the atmosphere inside the nest becomes too dry or hot.

This well-maintained environment is the perfect place for the monitor lizard to lay her eggs, so she will rip a hole in the nest with her powerful claws, and deposit her eggs in the very centre of the nest. Then, she simply leaves. The termites immediately begin rebuilding the nest, as a change in temperature can be disastrous for their young. Within hours, the broken walls will have been repaired, and the nest's temperature and humidity restored to proper levels. The termites seem oblivious to the lizard's eggs, sitting in the heart of their nest.

After a few months, the eggs hatch, and the young monitor lizards struggle free of their shells. However, they are too big to climb out of the termites' tunnels, so they have either to dig their way out or wait for their mother to come and break the nest open again.

Which animals make the best parents?

We have now heard many stories of cruel, negligent, and vicious animal parents, but what about the heroes of animal parenthood? Which parent offers the most caring, nurturing environment for its young? Is it the male Emperor penguin, who spends the winter in the frozen Antarctic, huddled with his brothers, each balancing a single, precious egg on the top of his feet? Or is it perhaps the female Australian social spider, who makes the ultimate sacrifice, allowing her young to feast on her body, killing her in the process?

Well, perhaps one way of measuring a parent's performance is to see how long the family unit stays together – if the young remain by their parents' side for a long time, it's a fair bet that they're being well looked after. Based on this criterion, the clear winner would seem to be the killer whale, which is also called an orca. Killer whales form the most stable family groups of all the mammals. Astonishingly, after twenty-five years of intensive research, watching killer whales in the coastal waters of the north-eastern Pacific Ocean, researchers have not observed one single incidence of a killer whale ever leaving its mother. As far as we know, every killer whale stays with its family group for the whole of its life.

CHAPTER THREE

Crafty creatures

Which creature can drop its tail off?

Many types of lizard, including skinks, have the ability to drop off their tails when threatened by a predator. Their tails have special fracture points, so that if they are being chased or grabbed by a predator, their tail will drop off. Amazingly, the tail will carry on wriggling for several minutes, confusing the predator, and creating the illusion of a continued struggle. With luck, this should buy the lizard enough time to escape.

In the weeks after losing one tail, the lizard will usually be able to grow another, although this one will contain cartilage rather than bone, and will often be smaller than the original tail. However, sometimes, if the first tail doesn't drop off fully, the new tail will grow alongside it, giving the lizard the freaky appearance of having two tails.

Glass lizards do something even more amazing. Like skinks, they drop off their tails when threatened, but when a glass lizard's tail drops off, it breaks into a number of pieces, shattering like glass. A glass lizard's tail makes up as much as two-thirds of the creature's length, so, when it drops off and shatters, it makes a shocking and extraordinary sight, since it looks as if the creature has spontaneously smashed into pieces, which technically it has. Often, the broken pieces of the tail will continue to twitch, while the glass lizard itself remains motionless, confusing and distracting the predator, and helping the lizard to make its escape.

Why do moles squeeze earthworms?

Moles are cute, furry, burrowing mammals, which are around 15 centimetres (6 inches) long, and weigh just 100 grams (3.5 ounces). They spend most of their lives foraging in a network of underground tunnels, through which they burrow at incredible speed. Moles have short, powerful legs, and very broad front feet, which they use for digging. Just one small mole can dig its way through an amazing 14 metres (46 feet) of soil in just one hour.

Moles have an active, high-energy lifestyle, which means they usually need to eat their own weight in food each day. Their diet can include insects, spiders, grubs, and even an occasional mouse, if it comes too close, but their main foodstuff is earthworms. When it finds an earthworm, a mole will pull it through its paws, squeezing it tightly, to force out any earth and mud from the earthworm's guts.

Then, the mole will either eat the worm, or keep it for later. Moles have a toxin in their saliva that can paralyse earthworms, so they will often bite off the earthworm's head, paralysing the worm but not killing it. They then store it in their specially constructed underground larder. Scientists have found well-stocked mole larders containing as many as a thousand paralysed earthworms.

How do fireflies tell fire-lies?

Fireflies are celebrated for their wonderful ability to produce cold light (meaning that there is no heat emitted), through a process called bioluminescence, in which the light is produced by the reaction of two chemicals in the presence of oxygen. Female fireflies use these green, yellow, and pale-red lights to attract a mate. They flash their lights in a distinct pattern which is unique to their species, and acts as a signal to nearby males. This system helps the males and females of each species to find eligible partners, and to avoid wasting time paying visits to fireflies of other species.

However, some crafty female fireflies have found a way to subvert this system. Photuris fireflies, which are also known as 'femme fatale fireflies', can copy the flash patterns of other species, attracting males of this species. When the male flies down, he is expecting to find a friendly and receptive female of his own species. Instead, however, he finds a hungry femme fatale, who quickly kills him and eats him for dinner.

Which spider looks like a blob of bird poo?

There is a spider, appropriately known as the bird-dropping spider, that looks just like a lump of bird poo. It has a grey and white body, and it is usually found with its legs tucked in, curled up in a ball, sitting on a leaf, just where a blob of bird muck might land. It may not be pretty, but this disguise is far from unique, as there are also a number of caterpillars which use a similar camouflage.

Why would any creature choose to look like bird poo? Well, first it protects them from predators, as this spider's most likely attackers are birds, who naturally avoid eating the faeces of other birds. Second, it helps them hunt food of their own, as the spider's prey are unlikely to see any threat in the common sight of a splodge of bird mess, and so may come far closer than is good for them.

Which spider hunts like a gaucho?

Gauchos were South American cowboys, who used a special technique for bringing down cattle. They used a throwing weapon called a bolas, which consisted of a piece of rope with wooden or metal balls at each end, and another ball tied to the middle. Gauchos would throw these weapons with great skill at the legs of fleeing cattle, tying up their legs, and making them trip and fall.

In many parts of the world, including South America, lives a spider that amazingly uses a similar technique to snare its prey. The bolas spider is about the size of a pea, and coloured black and white. When darkness starts to fall, the spider goes hunting. First, it lays a line of non-sticky silk on the under-side of a twig or leaf. Then, it hangs from this line, using two of its legs. Next, it spins a line of sticky silk, about a couple of centimetres long, with a sticky blob of silk at the end, like the weighted end of the bolas. Now, the spider simply hangs there, dangling its line, which glints in the twilight. It will stay like this for up to fifteen minutes, and, if it hasn't caught anything by then, it will reel in its line and eat it, perhaps because the line will have lost its stickiness.

In these first few hours of the night, the spider is hunt-ing for cutworm moths. Eventually one will appear, flying straight for the spider's dangling line. The moth may be attracted by the light glinting off the sticky silk. It is also attracted by the pheromones that the spider emits, which are an exact chemical match for the perfume used in cut-worm moth courtship. As the moth gets closer, the spider swishes the bolas, swiping the moth into its mouth.

A few hours later, these moths are no longer active, so the spider pulls in the line, eats it, and takes a rest. At midnight, it goes hunting again, but this time it has a new target: a moth called the smoky tetanolita. Amazingly, the spider now begins to produce a different pheromone, this one designed to attract its new prey, like a skilful fisherman varying his bait to attract a different type of fish.

Which spider builds a life-size model of itself?

Many types of spider decorate their webs, and these decorations seem to serve a number of functions. Some spiders use silk ornaments to strengthen the web. Other decorations seem designed to make the web more visible, either to deter large animals from accidentally walking into the web and destroying it, or to attract prey. However, scientists in Taiwan have recently discovered a fascinating and unique use of web decoration, after observing one type of spider building a life-size replica of itself as a decoy to fool predators. No other creature is known to build a model of itself in this way.

A number of species of orb spider are known to decorate their webs with various types of material, including discarded eggs sacs, plant matter, and the remains of prey. Until recently, this kind of decoration was believed to be used as camouflage. However, scientists observing the spiders found that wasps were actually more likely to attack decorated webs than plain ones, suggesting that the decorations could serve no useful purpose as camouflage.

Observing another species of orb spider, *Cyclosa mulmeinensis*, on Orchid Island off the south-east coast of Taiwan, the scientists noticed that when decorating its web, it built pellets using eggs sacs and dead insect bodies that were exactly the same size and shape as its own body, and that would appear to wasps to be the same colour as the spider's body, and to reflect light in the same way. When wasps attacked the web, more often than not they would attack the decoy rather than the spider, suggesting that while these decoys might attract more wasps than an undecorated web, they nonetheless made the spider safer overall.

Do fish fish for fish?

There's a type of fish that has a very crafty technique for catching its prey. It is called an anglerfish, because it attracts its prey using bait just like a fisherman. However, the prey it uses is its own tongue, which is long and thin, and wriggles like a worm. The anglerfish sits on a reef, with its mouth wide open, and its tongue wriggling, looking just like a juicy, tasty worm. When a curious fish comes closer, looking for a snack, instead it finds itself being sucked into the anglerfish's mouth, and becoming a snack itself.

The anglerfish is the only fish that is known to use this technique, but there is also a kind of turtle that does something very similar. The alligator snapping turtle is a big, ferocious predator, which can weigh as much as 100 kilograms (220 pounds). Its jaws are hooked, and have a sharp cutting edge made of horn. It is so fierce that if you approach one on land it may well attack you. It is perhaps justified in being confident in its strength, since it and its near relatives have proven to be one of the most resilient and enduring life forms on Earth. The alligator snapping turtle is a close descendant of an ancient tortoise called *Triassochelys*, or the Triassic turtle, whose remains have been found in rocks of Triassic age, from around 245 million years ago.

The alligator snapping turtle lies at the bottom of lakes with its mouth open, using its tongue to tempt passing fish. Like the anglerfish, the snapping turtle has a long, thin, bright red tongue, which wriggles in such a way as to perfectly mimic a worm. However, the turtle's technique is slightly different from that of the anglerfish. Instead of sucking its prey into its mouth, it snaps its powerful jaws shut, often chopping the fish in half.

How do Japanese crows crack open walnuts?

Carrion crows are found throughout the forests of Japan. These forests produce an abundance of walnuts, which could make a tasty and nutritious treat, but until recently carrion crows have never been able to crack them open, because their beaks are not strong enough. Many birds do manage to crack open similarly obstinate foodstuffs by dropping them from the air – for example, bearded vultures live mainly on a diet of bone marrow, which they get by dropping bones from a great height, cracking them open.

The similarly ingenious Egyptian vulture likes to eat ostrich eggs, which are full of nutrients, but their shells are very thick and difficult to crack open. The solution these vultures have discovered is to drop rocks onto the eggs, breaking the shells. Walnuts too can be cracked open by being dropped, but they have to be dropped as many as fifty times, so it's a lot of work for a small snack.

However, in 1990 the ingenious carrion crows of Sendai City came up with an impressive solution. They started using cars. The birds wait at the city's traffic lights, holding a walnut in their beaks. When the lights turn red, they swoop down and place the nut in front of a car's tyres. When the lights turn green, the cars drive over the nuts, cracking them open. The birds wait for the lights to turn red again, and then hop back down into the road, and pick up their dinner. This behaviour is slowly spreading, as other crows observe it happening, and then take it up themselves. One of the most fascinating aspects of this behaviour is that the crows seem to have learned to use traffic lights, and to understand something of how they work, as other stretches of road would be too dangerous.

Why do birds feign injury?

There are a number of birds, such as lapwings and plovers, that, rather than building elaborate nests in trees, simply lay their eggs on open ground – on marshes, grasslands, or beaches. This is a simpler solution than building an elabo-rate nest, but it means the eggs are more vulnerable to predators such as foxes. One way to protect the eggs is to camouflage them, and so birds that nest in this way tend to produce eggs with mottled patterns, to make them invisible against the gravelly ground. When the chicks hatch, the parent birds carry away the broken bits of shell, so that their shiny white interiors don't reveal the location of the nest.

Nonetheless, this camouflage is an imperfect solution. If a predator gets close to the nest, it is unlikely to be deceived, so the mother will try a different trick: she will feign injury, to distract the predator from the nest. When a predator approaches, lapwings and plovers hop away from their nests, dragging a wing along the ground, as if they are hurt. To ensure that they attract the predator's attention, they may start screaming, as if in pain or distress.

A predator such as a stoat is likely to be far more tempted by the prospect of a fully grown adult bird than a handful of eggs or chicks, and so it follows, getting gradually dragged away from the location of the nest. As the predator gets closer to the mother, at the last minute she suddenly flies away, as if she has been miraculously healed. However, the stoat has by now been led so far away from the nest that, even if it had spotted the eggs in the first place, it now has no way of retracing its steps and finding them again, particularly given the kind of nondescript, uniform landscapes where these birds nest, such as marshes and shingle beaches.

Other birds seem to have developed this trick to an even more advanced degree. Instead of feigning injury, purple sandpipers on the Arctic tundra run away from their nests with both wings trailing behind, raising their feathers, while making a squeaking sound that bears no resemblance to their usual calls. The effect of this is that they look and sound just like a scuttling mouse or lemming, both of which are particularly tempting prey for Arctic foxes, who are the most likely audience for this performance. In the United States, the green-tailed towhee also tries to mimic another kind of appealing prey. If a coyote approaches, it will run from its nest while lifting its tail, which at first glance makes it look a bit like a chipmunk, which is the main prey of local coyotes.

Do animals tell lies?

A number of species of bird are known to deceive one another for their own gain, taking advantage of the communal sentinel system by which many birds depend on one another for their safety. Often an area of woodland or forest will contain many species of bird of a similar size, which will all be similarly threatened by the arrival of a larger predator such as a hawk. Consequently, birds have developed a wonderfully resourceful sentinel system, in which the first bird to spot the danger will sound the alarm, by giving a particular type of call, which is usually written as 'seet'. It is a soft, short, high-pitched call, which is clear and easily understood, but difficult to locate, thus minimising the danger for the sentinel. Obviously, an alarm call that significantly endangered the signaller would be of very limited value. Many hedgerow birds, including finches, thrushes and tits, use a seet call, which is simultaneously understood by birds of different species, like an international language. On hearing the seet call, all the birds in the area will drop what they are doing, find shelter, and remain quiet.

However, this system also presents opportunities for deception. In the Amazonian rainforest, communities of small birds operate a sentinel system, while they rummage through the leaf litter looking for tasty insects. Here, two species of bird often act as sentinels: antshrikes, which keep watch under the shade of the canopy; and shrike tanagers, which act as lookouts above the canopy. Doing this job means that these birds have less time to forage for insects, so the other birds reward them by letting them have some of the insects that they find. However, sometimes the sentinels will lie. If they spot a particularly tasty-looking insect being dug up, they may give a warning call, even though there is no actual danger. The other birds will flee for safety, and the sentinel will come and grab the insect.

A number of monkey species use a similar system of alarm calls. Vervet monkeys have at least five different calls, which give detailed warnings as to which direction the danger is coming from, whether it is from the ground or the air, and how urgent and threatening the danger is. Again, however, sometimes the sentinels tell lies. In one example, researchers witnessed one monkey watching another monkey digging up a large root. Just as the digger was about to pull this tempting prize from the ground, the sentinel shouted the alarm for 'snake', which sent the other monkey scuttling up into the trees for safety. Then, the crafty lookout came down and grabbed the tasty root, with no snake in sight.

In a more detailed study, capuchin monkeys were found to do the same thing. In an Argentinian national park, scientists found that the monkeys sounded alarm calls ten times more frequently when pieces of banana were placed in the open. In other words, when there was a tasty incentive to send the other monkeys fleeing for safety, the sentinel monkeys were much more likely to give an alarm call, even though the level of danger was constant.

Of course, the two main preoccupations of most creatures are food and reproduction, and so, as we might expect, there are also examples of animals telling lies for the purpose of attracting a mate. Male domestic chickens, for example, are known to produce a specific type of call when they have found food, in order to tempt a female. However, sometimes these chickens give this call deceptively, even though in fact they have no food, purely to try to lure the female to come closer.

Which bird is an expert impressionist?

In the forests of southern Australia lives a bird with an extraordinary talent. It is the male Australian lyrebird, and it sings one of the most beautiful and complex songs of any bird. When it is time to mate, the female lyrebirds make a tour of the males' display mounds in the forest, to inspect their potential partners. The males are extraordinary looking, with cream-coloured, fanlike tail feathers.

When the males display, they bend these tail feathers forward, completely covering themselves.

At the same time, they sing an incredible song, or rather a variety of songs, which are not only pleasing to the ear, but are also full of clever mimicry and references. The male lyrebird's courtship song incorporates an amazing variety of trills and warbles, as well as mimicking the songs of almost every other bird in the neighbouring area. Ornithologists are said to be able to recognise the calls of more than a dozen different birds in the lyrebird's repertoire. Presumably, this amazing talent has evolved in response to the female's desire for ever more complex and varied aural stimulation.

Perhaps the most impressive aspect of the lyrebird's performance is that these songs are not just inherited traits, passed down through the generations. Rather, each individual bird has a talent for spontaneous mimicry, and can quickly learn and incorporate new sounds. This is demonstrated by the amazing speed with which these birds incorporate the sounds of human activity into their songs, when their territories are close to human settlements. Lyre-birds observed near populated areas have been known to incorporate the sounds of chainsaws, car alarms, barking dogs, camera motors, car horns, welding machines, and crying babies into their recitals. Some are also said to have learned tunes that they've overheard being played by musicians.

Why do owls collect poo?

A large proportion of a burrowing owl's diet consists of dung beetles, and so these wise old birds have come up with an ingenious way to attract their prey. Dung beetles, of course, love nothing more than poo; in fact, their whole society is based on it. Taking advantage of this, burrowing owls collect the droppings of cows, horses and other large mammals, and carry them back to their burrows, lining their nests with the smelly stuff. This bait is enough to attract the dung beetles, who scuttle their way to the burrow's entrance, hoping for a tasty meal. Instead, they soon find that the hungry owl waiting there deserves its reputation for intelligence.

Which bird turns itself into a parasol?

Green-backed herons are perhaps the craftiest fishermen of all the birds, as they use a number of sophisticated techniques to catch their prey, and are also able to quickly learn new tricks. One of the heron's clever techniques is to turn itself into a parasol. On a hot day, a wading heron may spread its broad wings, creating a patch of cool shady water in the lake or river where it is hunting. Remaining quite still, the heron then waits for a fish to swim into this pleasant patch of shade, before grabbing it in its beak.

However, this is only one of this particular heron's impressive range of fishing techniques. In Japan, green-backed herons seem to have recently learned to fish with bait, having presumably picked up the habit from observing humans. In a public park, where people come to feed the exotic fish, herons have started picking up morsels of bread, and dropping them on to the surface of the lake, as if feeding the fish. When a hungry fish comes to the surface to take the bread, the heron grabs it in its beak. Herons have also been seen using insects as bait in the same way.

The heron also uses another, even more sophisticated tactic. As fishermen will tell you, fish are naturally inquisitive. It is not always necessary to offer food to get them to rise to the surface; something shiny or colourful will do the trick just as well. A bird called the little egret attracts fish in this way. It has black legs with bright yellow feet. To attract fish, the little egret shakes one of its brightly coloured feet on the surface of the water, tempting fish to come and investigate. The green-backed heron has also learned to do something similar, dangling small feathers on the water's surface, and this also seems to work.

Which bird can chat with badgers?

The honeyguide is a small, dull-looking bird, distantly related to woodpeckers, which is found in Asia and Africa. Despite the name, it isn't really honey that the honeyguide likes to eat. Rather, it eats bee larvae and bees' wax, as well as other insects. In fact, it is the only animal of any kind that is known to be able to digest wax. In Asia, bees tend to nest in relatively open, unprotected sites, such as hanging from the ceiling of a cave. Honeyguides have no trouble raiding these nests.

However, African bees tend to choose more secluded, inaccessible sites for their nests, such as in holes in trees, or hidden between rocks. Honeyguides can't get to these nests, so they recruit the help of a creature called a honey badger, which is also known as a ratel. Ratels do love honey, and they have the necessary claws and physical strength to break into the kind of secluded nests that honeyguides are adept at finding, but unable to crack open. Amazingly, these two very different species have learned to work together, in a mutually beneficial partnership.

When the honeyguide finds a ratel, it will perch nearby and call to it, giving a distinctive, chattering cry. The ratel will answer with a series of guttural growls, and begin to follow the bird. The honeyguide flies off, frequently stopping, calling and fluttering its tail at the ratel, to make sure it's still following, while the ratel answers these calls by growling back. Eventually the bird reaches the hive, and it communicates this to the ratel by climbing up to a higher perch and giving a different call. The ratel apparently understands what this means – that the nest is nearby – and so it begins digging for it. Once the ratel finds the nest, the bees attack it, swarming around its head and stinging it, but it responds by farting into the nesthole, and the smell it produces is apparently as unbearable to bees as it is to humans, as most of the bees now flee. Using its claws, the ratel tears out the honeycombs, and carries them away. The honeyguide now swoops down to forage in what's left of the wreckage of the nest, feasting on the dead bees, grubs, and honeycomb.

Furthermore, ratels are not the only animals that honeyguides have learned to work with. They also collaborate with humans, specifically the Boran people of East Africa. When they want to find some honey, the Boran bushmen will give a specific whistle, known as a *fuulido*, to summon the honeyguide, which will then lead them to a secluded bees' nest, just like it would lead a ratel. According to tradition, once the bushmen are finished, they leave a gift of honey for the honeyguide, to thank it for its help.

What is the natural world's most unlikely impressionist?

One candidate must be the tiny blister beetle larva, which manages to impersonate a creature hundreds of times its size. Or, rather, it manages to do so collectively, with the help of hundreds of its siblings. Blister beetles are found in the Mojave Desert in the western United States. The females lay their eggs on the sand, where they hatch as tiny, hairy, black larvae, which look nothing like their parents, or indeed like any other beetle. These larvae stick together as a group, and climb the nearest grass stem, where they huddle together as a single, shiny mass. This mass looks roughly the same size and shape as a female digger bee, although to our eyes there would seem to be only a limited resemblance. They also emit the same chemical pheromone as a receptive female digger bee.

Within minutes, this impersonation is usually good enough to attract a male digger bee, which will come in to land on the group, and attempt to mate with them. At this moment, they suddenly disperse, and climb onto his body, gripping him with their tiny claws.

At this point, the male flies off, no doubt somewhat baffled at the sudden disappearance of his intended mate, but apparently unaware that he's now wearing what looks like a dinner jacket made of tiny black beetle larvae. With luck, however, he soon finds another female, and this one may even be a real bee. As he lands on her, ready to begin copulation, the beetle larvae quickly transfer themselves onto her body. They are now on the home stretch of their unlikely journey. The fertilised female now returns to her nest, where she has filled a number of open cells with pollen. Here, the beetle larvae dismount, to enjoy their new home, where they will grow in safety, feasting on the bees' eggs and honey, before emerging as adult blister beetles.

How do stick insects get ants to incubate their eggs?

Stick insects like to keep things simple. Often, female stick insects don't even bother involving the male in the business of reproduction. Instead, a female will simply produce eggs all by herself, in a process of asexual reproduction called 'parthenogenesis', in other words genesis with no Pa. Then, rather than caring for the eggs, the stick insect mother simply lets them drop to the ground. However, despite this apparently lax approach to child rearing, the species endures, thanks to a number of cunningly designed evolutionary traits.

In Australia, one species of stick insect, called the spiny leaf insect, feeds almost exclusively on the leaves of the casuarina tree. These trees produce small, fleshy seeds that are rich in oil and nutrients. For this reason, harvester ants collect these seeds, which they store safely in their nests, ready to be eaten. The female spiny leaf insect takes advantage of this, by producing eggs that are small, round and finely ridged, exactly like casuarina seeds. The harvester ants can't tell the difference, so they collect the insect's eggs along with the seeds, and store them all together. Later, when the ants come to eat their stores, they find that only some of the seeds have sprouted tasty attachments, so they leave the eggs alone, where they grow in safety underground.

Eventually, the eggs hatch, and we might imagine that this would put the infant stick insects in considerable danger. They are, after all, uninvited intruders in the ants' nest. However, the stick insect's gift for mimicry protects the infants once again, since, when they hatch, they look and move exactly like newborn ants. Consequently, the ants allow them to walk out of the nest unmolested, after which they climb up the casuarina tree to start the process again.

Are sheep as dumb as they look?

Well, it's true that sheep don't possess the most dazzling intellects of the animal kingdom, but they perhaps deserve more credit than they are given. For one thing, they have excellent memories. They can remember the faces of sheep and people for up for two years. They can also be trained to remember the rocks and streams that mark the boundaries of their territory, and then pass on this information to their young. This is obviously an extremely useful trait from a shepherd's point of view, and incredibly flocks of sheep will retain this information for centuries, passing it down from one generation to the next.

Sheep have also displayed some rather more daring talents. Recently, for example, sheep in Yorkshire have taught themselves how to roll across cattle grids, to raid the local villagers' gardens. Daredevil sheep have been observed taking a long run-up, and then rolling across the hoof-proof grids in a ball, like an SAS commando. Since these grids are about 2.5 metres (8 feet) wide, this is no mean feat. The hungry sheep are also said to have learned to climb or hurdle over fences up to 1.5 metres (5 feet) high. So you see, not all sheep are sheepish!

How do stoats hypnotise rabbits?

Stoats are one of the animal kingdom's most extraordinary predators. They eat a varied diet, including birds, eggs, insects and small mammals. They hunt rabbits, even though rabbits are much bigger than stoats, and can weigh ten times as much. Rabbits are also strong, alert, agile and very fast, which makes them an extremely difficult meal to catch. However, stoats have an amazing technique to circumvent all these problems, without even having to chase the rabbit. Instead, they hypnotise it.

The stoat does this by stealthily approaching the rabbit, creeping towards it through the long grass. When it gets within range, it deliberately draws attention to itself, dancing, jumping and chasing its tail. It is a bizarre performance. The stoat somersaults, then backflips. It vanishes into the grass, then leaps up in the air again. The rabbit is mesmerised, as the dancing stoat gradually gets closer and closer. Suddenly, the stoat leaps towards the rabbit, and bites into the back of its neck, smashing the back of its skull with its teeth. The rabbit may twitch once or twice, before collapsing, dead. Biting into the rabbit's skull in this way not only ensures a quick death, but also minimises the risk that the meat will spoil, since a big rabbit will provide food for days. The businesslike stoat now drags the heavy corpse back to its burrow.

Which bird builds a decoy nest?

In the Australian bush, a type of bird called the splendid fairy wren is terrorised by currawongs, which are big, aggressive birds that destroy the fairy wrens' nests, and steal their eggs. The wrens have no way of defending themselves. All they can do is produce a huge number of eggs, in the hope that a few chicks will manage to survive this threat. Luckily, fairy wrens are extremely promiscuous and extremely fertile.

However, another bird that lives alongside the fairy wren has a different strategy. Yellow-rumped thornbills are about the same size as fairy wrens, and are therefore similarly threatened by the marauding currawongs. Their solution is to build a second, decoy nest, on top of the active one. The decoy nest is simply a cup-shaped depression, while underneath it sits the real nest, with a concealed entrance. Currawongs attack from above, so if they see the empty decoy nest, they are likely to leave it alone and move on without investigating further, unaware of the active nest underneath. Thanks to this clever construction, thornbill nests suffer far less from currawong raids than those of their wanton neighbours.

How do squirrels deceive rattlesnakes?

A squirrel's tail is one of the most versatile tools of any mammal. Squirrels use their tails to balance when walking along a precarious branch. If they do fall, their tail acts as a parachute, catching the air, and slowing the squirrel's descent. When running on the ground, squirrels use their tails as a fifth limb and rudder, to help them change direction at speed. If a bird should attack, a squirrel can shelter under its big bushy tail, making it impossible for the bird to grab it in its talons. In the summer, a tail makes an effective sunshade; while in the winter, it's a wonderfully soft, warming duvet, which helps the squirrel to conserve precious heat and energy.

However, another exciting use for the squirrel's tail has

recently been discovered. Snakes are one of the squirrel's most dangerous predators, but squirrels have found a way to use their tails to protect themselves against one group, namely rattlesnakes. Rattlesnakes have a poor sense of sight, but they have another way of 'seeing' their prey, using their extremely sensitive heat-sensing organs. These organs consist of two small pits, one at either side of the snake's head, between its eyes and its nostrils. These pits can detect infrared radiation so accurately that the snake can tell the size, shape, distance, and direction of prey, purely from sensing its heat energy, which it can observe at as little as 0.2 degrees Celsius above the background temperature.

When a squirrel is confronted by a rattlesnake, it fills its tail with blood, raising the tail's temperature. Since the rattlesnake can only really see things if they are warm, this makes the squirrel look twice as big as it otherwise would, which can be enough to make the rattlesnake warily slink off, leaving the squirrel in peace. What is most amazing about this ingenious technique is that squirrels don't bother to heat up their tails for other snakes. They do it only for snakes such as rattlesnakes that have these heat-sensing organs.

What is particularly devious about the Alcon Blue butterfly?

The Alcon Blue butterfly (*Maculinea alcon*) is an extremely attractive specimen, which is found in Europe and northern Asia, where it brightens up many a summer's afternoon. However, as delicate and charming as they look, Alcon Blues are one of nature's most devious schemers, when it comes to raising their young.

The process begins when the butterfly lays its eggs on the leaves of a gentian plant. When the caterpillars hatch from the eggs, they burrow into the gentian buds and feed. During this time, they become much larger, before eventually dropping to the ground. Here, the caterpillar is found by ants. At this point, the caterpillar begins to produce a chemical pheromone, which somehow seems to induce the worker ants to treat it like one of their own precious larvae. The ants take the caterpillar back to their nest, and begin to feed it.

However, the caterpillar is not satisfied with food and safe lodgings. Now, its chemical signals instruct the ants to give it preferential treatment. If the nest is disturbed, the ants will rush the caterpillar to safety, while ignoring their own young. For an astonishing two years, the ants will continue to feed the interloper until it is fully grown, and ready to take its adult form. When it emerges from its pupal stage, the butterfly is at last recognised for the impostor that it is, but by this point the ants' attacks are futile, since they are unable to grab the butterfly's adult scales.

However, this story of deception and intrigue has one more amazing twist. The butterfly does not always make it to its adult stage, because another crafty creature may further complicate things. While the Alcon Blue is still a caterpillar, a female ichneumon wasp may appear. These parasitic wasps seem to be able to sense when an ants' and is hosting an Alcon Blue. The wasp enters the nest, and the ants panic and try to attack her. In response, she emits an amazing pheromone of her own, which not only repels the ants from her, but also makes them attack one another. In the confusion, she lands on the caterpillar, and injects an egg deep inside its body.

After the wasp flies off, the ants continue life as normal. They feed the caterpillar as assiduously as always, and it eventually turns into a chrysalis. However, when the chrysalis opens, it's not an Alcon Blue butterfly that emerges, but an ichneumon wasp, which has devoured the butterfly pupa from the inside out!

Why do male cuttlefish pretend to be female?

Despite their name, cuttlefish are not actually fish. Instead, they are molluscs, from the same class as squid and octopuses. And, just like squid and octopuses, cuttlefish are masters of disguise, able to change their shape, colour and texture to evade predators, or to sneak up on prey of their own.

They also use these amazing talents in their elaborate courtship displays. Australian giant cuttlefish lead a mostly solitary life, but every winter they come together at Spencer Gulf off the coast of South Australia to mate. There may be as many as eleven males for every female, which means there is considerable competition for partners. Consequently, the cuttlefish use a range of tactics to try to win a mate. Groups of males cluster around a female, jostling for position. The dominant males are those that are biggest and most colourful, so most of the males compete by trying to appear fierce, and by producing amazing displays of rippling colours, which travel in waves down their bodies.

However, the smaller males are unlikely to succeed in this type of competition, so they employ craftier tactics. Sometimes, while the bigger males are fighting for position, a smaller male will appear from behind a rock, and sneak in to mate with the female. Naturally enough, he is known as the 'sneaker male'.

Some males even pretend to be female themselves, to distract and confuse their rivals. They do this by pulling their arms in, and producing mottled colours on their back, which makes them look just like a female cuttlefish. Usually, this will lure some of the males, drawing them away from a real female. At just the right moment, the crafty cross-dresser will then dart back through the pack of males, and mate with the real female, before they realise that they've been fooled.

Cuttlefish are not the only creatures to have discovered the benefits of embracing their feminine side. Young male garter snakes also pretend to be female, to outwit rival males. Garter snakes can't change colour, but the males and females produce pheromones that are distinctive enough to make them instantly distinguishable from one another. However, young males also produce female pheromones, which serve to attract older males, who then attempt to mate with the young impostors. All male garter snakes go through this 'cross-dressing' phase in their youth, and it may help them to gain an advantage over their older rivals. If the older male is tricked into trying to mate with a young impostor, his chances of being able to mate with a real female will be substantially reduced.

Some birds use a similar strategy, albeit for a slightly different purpose. Male common terns try to attract a female by flying with a fish in their beak, hoping a female will follow. If he manages to tempt a female, the male tern will offer her the fish in midair. The pair then glide to the ground together, where he struts for her benefit, in a courtship display. However, some male common terns will pretend to be female, and follow their unwitting rival, purely so that they can nab a free dinner.

CHAPTER FOUR

Beastly blunders

Why is global warming so potentially disastrous for crocodiles?

Global warming has potentially disastrous consequences for any number of animal species. According to a recent study carried out by the United Nations, an increase in the average global temperature of more than 2.5 per cent would put 20–30 per cent of known species at increased risk of extinction. Of these, crocodilians – a group that includes crocodiles, alligators, gharials and caimans – are threatened in a particularly direct way, which could wipe out many species within just a few generations.

The reason for this arises from the unusual way in which the sex of young crocodilians is determined. In birds and mammals, males produce two different types of sperm. One contains a chromosome that determines that the fertilised egg will produce a male, while the other kind produces a female. Therefore, the sex of the young is decided at the moment the egg is fertilised. In crocodilians, on the other hand, the sex of the egg is not determined until much later in the process, and the deciding factor is the temperature at which the eggs are kept.

In laboratory tests, it has been found that crocodilian eggs, if kept in incubators at 32–34 degrees Celsius, will all produce male young. If the eggs are kept at a cooler temperature, of between 28 and 31 degrees Celsius, all the eggs will develop into females. If the temperature is some-where between the two, at 31–32 degrees Celsius, the eggs will produce a mixture of males and females, with the ratio depending on the species. A fraction of a degree can make a huge difference to the ratio of males to females that are produced. Even the relatively mild fluctuations of an un-usually hot or mild season can cause a significant imbalance in the ratio of the genders. The fear, therefore, is that the kind of rise in average global temperature currently being forecast, of two degrees or more in the next century, could have disastrous consequences for crocodilian populations.

Do animals get depressed?

A number of animals do seem to suffer from stress-related illnesses and bouts of depression. Many social creatures respond negatively to being isolated, and parrots seem to find it particularly distressing. A parrot kept captive may begin to behave in odd ways, including plucking out its own feathers, injuring itself with its beak, and screaming. This kind of behaviour seems to be a response to confinement, boredom and loneliness. When kept in isolation for long periods, some larger parrots have even seemed to lose their sanity.

Dogs are also susceptible to anxiety and depression. Some vets have recently started giving dogs antidepressant drugs, since dog depression is believed to be very similar to human depression. The drug they use is a chewable antidepressant called Reconcile, which contains the same selective serotonin-reuptake inhibitor used in the human drug Prozac.

Ferrets can also suffer from stress and depression, particularly if they are kept apart from a regular companion. They exhibit obvious symptoms, such as refusing their meals, and moping around for weeks on end. Surprisingly perhaps, this tendency to gloom makes ferrets a soothing and therapeutic companion for people who are themselves ill or depressed. The theory is that the ferret's emotional nature makes it easier for us to empathise with them than with

other, sunnier pets, and so ferrets are used in pet therapy, helping the recoveries of human depression sufferers, as well as the elderly and infirm.

Do any animals commit suicide?

A number of creatures exhibit a range of suicidal behaviours, although whether any of these could be described as deliberate suicide is clearly beyond our understanding. Many mammals and birds will fight to the death to protect their young, even against impossible odds. Some spider mothers effectively feed themselves to their young, sacrificing their lives in the process. Common octopuses will feed their young at the expense of themselves, and sometimes starve to death as a result. Many insects that live in colonies, such as bees, ants and termites, will fight to the death to protect their hive or nest. Some species even produce soldiers who function as suicide bombers – when threatened by danger, they literally explode themselves, hampering the attacker by covering it in their sticky remains.

Other creatures can to be induced to commit suicide by parasites. A parasite called the Gordian worm can infect grasshoppers, crickets, beetles, cockroaches and crustaceans. Once it has infected its host, the parasite somehow affects the insect's brain, making it seek out water and drown itself, thus returning the worm to the water.

Another deadly parasite is a protozoan called *Toxoplasma gondii*, which is usually found in cats. However, it sometimes infects small mammals such as mice and rats, and when it does, it affects their behaviour in an amazing way. Somehow, the parasite manages to switch off their fear of cats, so that the rats and mice are instead drawn towards them. This effect is amazingly specific, since it doesn't alter the rodent's other natural fears, such as those of open spaces and unfamiliar food. But why would this strategy be useful for the parasite? The answer is that if the rodent gets eaten by a cat, the parasite will be able to sexually reproduce inside the cat, which is something it cannot do inside rodents.

Yet another parasite, called the lancet liver fluke, seems to force ants to commit suicide. The parasite lives and reproduces inside cattle and large mammals, and its eggs are expelled with the animal's faeces. A terrestrial snail may then eat the faeces, ingesting some of the eggs. These then hatch into parasite larvae, which drill through the wall of the snail's gut, into its digestive tract. The snail defends itself by forming a cyst around the larvae, which it then excretes. The next stage in the parasite's astonishing journey comes when an ant, following the snail's trail of moisture, will eat the cyst, thus becoming infected itself. Once inside the ant, the parasite begins to affect its actions. Each evening, the ant will remove itself from the rest of the colony, and climb to the top of a blade of grass, where it will remain until dawn. The next morning, if it has survived the night, it will return to its colony as normal, but that evening it will once again climb to the top of a blade of grass and wait there. Eventually, it will be eaten by a large grazing mammal, such as a cow, allowing the parasite's life cycle to begin again.

Of course, the most famous example of animal suicide is the story of lemmings leaping headlong over cliffs. Some aspects of this well-worn story are accurate, but the lemming's behaviour could not be described as suicide. The story begins with the lemming's reproductive cycle, which is incredibly rapid. Six days after mating, the female gives birth, and she will be able to do so again within a month. Each time, she gives birth to as many as a dozen young, and each of these becomes sexually mature within three weeks of being born. Lemmings are vegetarians, which means their food supplies rapidly increase during spring and summer, allowing the population to do the same. Consequently, by the beginning of autumn, a local lemming population may have exploded to 200 times what it was in the spring.

This kind of exponential growth cannot continue indefinitely. Usually, every four or five years, the lemmings will have exhausted local food supplies, and so the population crashes. However, every thirty or forty years, there is an even bigger population explosion, causing a tide of lemmings to surge downhill from the forests of Scandinavia. They swarm into people's homes and gardens, destroying the farmers' crops, and travelling as far as ten miles a day.

Individuals in this kind of throng obviously have very little choice as to their direction, so, when they reach a river or sea, the pressure of the mass may well force those at the front into the water. This may lead some of them to drown, if the body of water is too big to cross, as lemmings swim in a straight line, so if they dive into a sea, they're almost certainly doomed. Despite its cost to some individual lemmings, this behaviour is believed to be very useful for the species as a whole, because it can expand their range considerably. One lemming migration from northern Finland in 1902 resulted in the formation of colonies a hundred miles away, on the coast of the Baltic Sea.

What happened to the exploding toads of Hamburg?

In April 2005, strange reports started to come out of Hamburg in Germany. According to local people, toads around the local lake had begun to explode spontaneously, with as many as a thousand of them meeting this horrible fate in a matter of days. According to reports, the toads were seen crawling on the ground, as their bodies gradually swelled to bursting point, before exploding, propelling their entrails up to a metre into the air. Local people began to worry, and the authorities warned that children and dogs should be kept away from the lake. The lake itself was sealed off, and became known as the 'pond of death'.

So what was causing this bizarre phenomenon? Were local people imagining it? Was it some kind of elaborate hoax? Or was there a more logical explanation? Scientists speculated that the cause could be some unknown virus or fungus in the pond; there had been cases of foreign horses at a nearby racetrack becoming infected by a type of fungus. Other suggested explanations included the overuse of pesticides, and increased ultraviolet radiation caused by depletion of the ozone layer.

One of Germany's top experts on amphibians, Franz Mutschmann, decided to investigate. He began collecting the toads' carcasses and performing autopsies on them. He noticed that all of the toads were missing their livers, and that each had a precise circular incision on its back, small enough to be the work of a bird's beak. He concluded that crows were attacking the toads, tearing out their livers. In response, the toads would fill themselves with air, as a defensive mechanism. However, with a hole in their body, and no liver, filling themselves with air caused their blood vessels and lungs to rupture, sending their intestines flying into the air.

But why were the crows so picky, taking only the toads' livers, rather than eating the whole creature? The answer is that the liver is pretty much the only part of a toad worth eating, since their skins are poisonous. Crows are intelligent creatures, who are capable of observing and learning new behaviours. In this case, it seems that one crow had seen another tearing out and enjoying a toad liver, copied the behaviour, and then it quickly spread.

Why do green turtles swim 1,500 miles to breed?

A great number of the green turtles found in the Atlantic all hatched on a remote, tiny stretch of land in the middle of the ocean, called Ascension Island. Turtles breed here in their thousands, after which the hatchlings get carried by the ocean currents towards Brazil, where they live and feed for several years. However, when they mature, and it comes to their time to breed, they begin an extraordinary journey back to the island of their birth, a journey of 2,500 kilometres (1,553 miles).

Not only is this journey unfathomably long, it is also an incredible feat of navigation. Ascension Island is just seven miles long, a tiny sliver of land in the South Atlantic Ocean, and yet the turtles somehow manage to find it, although we don't know how. Many turtles even seem to seek out the exact beach where they themselves were hatched. Some believe the turtles can navigate by using the position of the sun, while others suggest that they may use the Earth's magnetic field.

Another theory holds that they can somehow taste or smell tiny amounts of chemicals in the ocean current, leaching from Ascension Island's volcanic lava. Scientists have tracked the turtles, and found that they followed a remarkably straight line between Ascension Island and Brazil.

Why are poison-dart frogs endangered?

The amazing poison-dart frogs of Central and South America produce some of the most toxic poisons of any animal. The frogs are so toxic that they have few predators, and consequently they have developed incredibly bright, vividly coloured skins, to catch the eye of a mate, and to alert any potential predator to the danger they pose.

The most lethal of them all is perhaps the golden poison frog, which is believed to be the world's most poisonous vertebrate. The frog is just 5 centimetres (2 inches) long, but it contains enough poison to kill between ten and twenty adult humans. The tiniest drop of this poison will disable a person's nervous system, causing their muscles to contract uncontrollably, leading to heart failure. Chickens and dogs have been killed simply by coming into contact with a paper towel that one of these frogs had walked across.

One might imagine that a creature with such amazing defensive attributes would face few dangers, and yet many species of poison-dart frog are actually endangered. Ironically, it seems that it may be the frogs' incredible toxicity that is actually proving their undoing. The indigenous people of the Amazon rainforest have learned to extract the frogs' poison, by catching them, roasting them on a spit, and collecting the poison as it drips from their skin. The resulting sticky paste is then used to tip their arrows for hunting trips or warfare.

Why do some insects turn themselves to mush?

Many insects go through a process called metamorphosis, during which their body's structure undergoes abrupt and conspicuous change. This metamorphosis commonly takes an insect from its larval stage to adulthood, sometimes with an inactive stage in between, during which the creature is known as a pupa or chrysalis.

While in this pupal stage, an insect will produce digestive juices, which break down most of its body cells, turning them into mush. This process of cell death is called histolysis. At this point, only a small number of the insect's cells remain intact, and it's these cells that will divide and develop into the insect's adult body features, such as wings, antennae and legs. While this is happening, these developmental cells feed on the mush, using it as fuel for the insect's growth.

Incredibly, in some species such as fungus gnats, the metamorphosis can produce two 'twin' adults from a single larva. This is called polyembryony.

Which beetle seeks out fire?

What would you do if there was a rampaging forest fire heading straight towards you? You'd probably want to get away as fast as possible. However, one bizarre little beetle does the opposite. The black jewel beetle, which is also known as the firebug, can sense the faintest whiff of a forest fire at great distances. And, when it gets the scent, it heads straight for the inferno.

The reason is that the black jewel beetle likes to make its home in charred trees, ideally as soon as possible after a fire. Most creatures either flee a fire or die, which means that a charred tree is likely to be free of any predators. This means that a hot, charred tree provides a haven where the black jewel beetle can mate recklessly, and lay its eggs in safety, without fear of predators or competition.

The way in which the jewel beetle senses a distant fire is fascinating, and not yet fully understood. The beetle has a tiny infrared sensor under one of its legs, which allows it to detect the faintest whiff of woodsmoke from as far as 80 kilometres (50 miles) away. Scientists are hoping to somehow harness this amazing technology to develop an early warning system for forest fires.

Why do elephants die of hunger?

Elephants graze on the open plains of Africa and Asia, eating a fibrous diet of grass and leaves. This wears down their teeth very quickly. Other animals with a similar diet face the same problem, which they deal with in a variety of ways. Rabbits, for example, have teeth with open roots, which carry on growing throughout their lives, to replace the constant wear at the other end.

However, elephants' teeth grow in a different way. Most mammals' teeth emerge vertically from the jaw, but elephants' teeth move horizontally. As the old teeth are worn away, the elephants' new molars emerge at the back of the jaw, and gradually push through to the front, until the old ones drop out. However, there is a limit to how many sets of teeth an elephant can produce. After its given number of pairs are worn out, the elephant is unable to produce any more teeth, and so, even if it is healthy and capable in all other respects, it has no way of chewing its food, and so it starves to death.

Elephants are not alone in this: kangaroos too have a limited number of sets of teeth. Kangaroos can only produce four pairs of molars. Once these are worn away, any kangaroo which has managed to survive all the other dangers faced by an ageing large mammal, will nonetheless die of starvation.

Do any animals take medicine?

A number of mammals have learned to self-medicate. Chimpanzees eat the bristly leaves of the *Aspilia* plant, which contains a special oil that kills the bacteria, intestinal worms and other parasites by which the chimps' stomachs can become infected. The chimps pluck off the plant's leaves, mash them up in their hands, and chew them before swallowing. The leaves have little or no nutritional value, so the only reason to eat them seems to be their medicinal value. This theory is supported by the fact that the chimps seem to actually find the taste bitter, because when they eat the leaves, they pull faces, and give other indications that they find the taste unpleasant.

In another example, Rwandan mountain gorillas travel to special parts of the forest where they eat fistfuls of the earth, which is rich in special minerals that their normal diet lacks. It's not just primates who self-medicate, either. In the Amazon rainforest, macaws seek out essential minerals, which they get by pecking at exposed banks of mineral clays. Sheep too have been shown to supplement their diet. When given a diet high in tannins and oxalic acid, which can cause digestive problems, sheep will actively choose foods that contain substances, such as sodium bicarbonate, that help to soothe acidosis. Furthermore, tests have shown that sheep with specific digestive problems will be more likely to select foods containing, respectively, sodium bentonite, polyethylene glycol, or dicalcium phosphate, choosing the specific medicine that will alleviate their condition.

Do any animals take drugs?

We've seen how animals can self-medicate, but what about recreational drugs? Well, in the USA and Mexico, there is a poisonous plant which is known as crazy weed or locoweed. Cows will eat it given the chance, and even encourage others to develop the habit. The effects of 'locoism', as the condition is known, are quite obvious. Cows become clumsy and start bumping into things. They take enormous, unnecessary leaps over small objects such as twigs. They may become disturbed and aggressive, charging at anyone who comes near. The weed contains an alkaloid substance called swainsonine, which makes the cows unable to break down glycoproteins. Over time, these proteins can build up and damage the cow's nervous system, making it behave strangely.

Alcohol may be legal, but it too is of course a recreational drug, and humans are not the only creatures who enjoy its effects. On the Caribbean island of St Kitts, the local vervet monkeys like to hang around near the tourist bars, and finish the leftover cocktails. Researchers have studied the monkeys' drinking habits, and found that they are remarkably similar to our own. The majority of the monkeys were observed to be social drinkers. These monkeys would drink in moderation, in company with others. They never drank before lunch, and preferred their alcohol diluted with fruit juice. There was also a small group of teetotallers, who never drank at all. Finally, there was a hard core of binge drinkers, who made up 5 per cent of the group. These would drink as much alcohol as they could get their hands on, preferably neat spirits. Then they would make a lot of noise, and start fights, before eventually passing out.

Why do cats hate water?

As anyone who's ever tried to bathe one will tell you, cats do not like water. The simple reason for this is that their fur is not designed to be soaked. Cat fur has a water-resistant top layer, which can cope fine with a shower of rain. However, if the cat gets drenched, its fur can become waterlogged, making it difficult to dry. A submerged cat faces a real risk of drowning, since a heavy, waterlogged coat makes it very difficult for a furry cat to stay afloat. Cats also struggle to maintain their body temperature if they get soaked. A cat's fur does not dry easily, and, all the time its fur is wet, the cat will be losing body heat. As a result, a wet cat may even suffer hypothermia.

However, there are some exceptions. A number of cat species that live in hot climates have evolved different types of fur, allowing them to take a cooling dip without risk of drowning or hypothermia. One example is the Turkish Van cat, which is found in the region around Lake Van in eastern Turkey. This cat's fur has lost its undercoat, and has a smooth texture like cashmere, making it water-resistant. Lions, tigers and jaguars are all also known to enjoy a refreshing swim.

Another cat even hunts in the water. In Southeast Asia, the fishing cat dives into the water to catch fish. It has also been observed attacking ducks from under the surface.

Some domestic cats can also be taught to enjoy water. Many pet owners report that their cat enjoys playing with a running tap, or a shower head – in this way, the cat can experiment with water in a playful, gradual way, without the risk of getting waterlogged. Also, cats that are regularly entered into cat shows will often be quite comfortable being frequently bathed. These cats are often bred to be show cats, so they get used to regular baths as kittens.

What happens if you turn a shark upside down?

Amazingly, if you turn a shark onto its back, it will become completely immobile. For some reason, an overturned shark goes into a coma-like state, which is called tonic immobility, for fifteen minutes, during which it remains totally unresponsive. Its dorsal fins straighten, and its breathing and muscle contractions become more steady and relaxed. No one knows the reason for this strange reaction, but even the scent of food is not enough to wake the shark once it is in this state.

Do whales and elephants have big brains? If so, why aren't they clever?

Whales and elephants do indeed have big brains. A human brain weighs about 1.5 kilograms (3.3 pounds), whereas the brains of elephants and whales are about five times this size. It is also true that big brains do roughly correlate with increased intelligence. Most of the animals that we consider intelligent, such as dogs and dolphins, have much bigger brains than creatures that appear to exhibit much lower intelligence, such as mice and worms.

However, size isn't everything. For example, Neanderthal man had a bigger brain than modern *Homo sapiens*, but no one would argue that he was more intelligent. Equally, although whales and elephants have big brains, their intelligence is demonstrably lower than that of humans.

This discrepancy can be partly explained by the brain's relative size to the body. A lot of a brain's nerve cells exist to deal with fairly rudimentary physical functions, such as sensing heat and pain, keeping the body warm, breathing, walking and so on. Bigger creatures have bigger bodies, and so need bigger brains just to deal with these functions. This is one reason why bigger animals have bigger brains.

However, taking into account our size, human beings' brains are much bigger than they need to be to carry out these routine functions. Our brains make up on average about 2.1 per cent of our body mass, which is an unusually high proportion. An elephant's brain may be much bigger than ours, but it makes up only 0.15 per cent of the creature's body mass. And the reason our brains are so much bigger in relative terms is that certain sections of the human brain are much more developed than they are in elephants, whales and other large mammals.

All mammal brains are made up of similar types of material. Brains contain nerve cells, or neurons, which are clustered together in regions. They also contain what are known as glial cells, which act as the connective tissue of the nervous system, insulating and supporting the neurons. Furthermore, the brains of mammal species tend to contain the same regions. They all contain a spinal cord and brainstem, with regions to control standard body functions such as breathing, body temperature, and blood pressure. They all have regions at the base of the brain that are used for learning to walk, run and jump. And they all have a region called the cerebrum, for learning and remembering. However, it is this region, specifically an area called the cerebral cortex, that is much more developed in humans than in other mammals, and it is this which seems to give us our greater level of intelligence. In general, the animals that we regard as intelligent are those that also have larger cerebral cortices.

Do animals enjoy pornography?

Of all the animals, monkeys are of course our closest cousins. We should perhaps not be surprised, therefore, if they share some of our vices. In an experiment with rhesus macaque monkeys, scientists found that the creatures would willingly 'pay', by forfeiting their usual treat of a glass of cherry juice, in return for the opportunity to look at pictures of the faces and bottoms of high-ranking females.

However, the monkeys were found to be rather picky about their choice of visual stimulation. They had no interest in looking at equivalent pictures of low-ranking females, and in fact they could only be persuaded to look at those pictures if they were bribed with an even larger glass of cherry juice.

Scientists have also attributed a recent boom in the birth rate of captive giant pandas to the use of pornography. The endangered animals have been regularly shown DVD footage of other pandas mating, and this has seemingly proved stimulating enough to encourage the captive pandas to do the same. Thanks to this novel approach, in 2006 more than thirty panda cubs were bred in captivity in China, compared with just twelve in 2005, and nine in 2000.

Why are anteaters scared of ants?

Surprisingly, anteaters are quite wary about the type of ant they will eat. When an anteater finds an ants' nest, it will slash it open with its claws, and then poke its curved snout inside. At this point, lots of angry ants will swarm out to defend the colony, but the anteater can defend itself against these attacks. It keeps the lids of its eyes shut, and these lids are particularly thick, precisely for this purpose. It also closes its nostrils, using special muscles. It pokes its long, black tongue into the mound, where it explores the now ruined architecture of the ants' home. Its tongue is covered in sticky saliva, which is produced by a special gland in its chest. Flicking this tongue in and out, it laps up a tasty meal of ants, which are swallowed whole, ready to be mashed up by the rough lining of the anteater's muscular stomach. In this way, a large anteater such as the giant African pangolin can eat as many as 200,000 insects in a single night.

However, despite its defensive abilities, the anteater will rarely stay at one colony for long. It will generally move away quickly, before the massed ranks of the colony's soldier ants pour out to attack the invader. Consequently, an anteater will rarely take more than a hundred or so insects from one nest.

Many anteaters, such as the South American tamandua, are also quite cautious about which species of ant they will eat. They avoid leaf-cutting ants, as these have powerful scissor-like jaws, which they use to cut leaf segments, but which they can also use on their enemies. They also avoid army ants, which have jaws strong enough to tear a scorpion apart. The tamandua prefers to seek out ants with less developed defensive mechanisms. They also regularly feed on tree termites, which have soft, tender bodies, and are not actually ants at all.

Why do rhinos charge into trees?

Rhinos have very poor eyesight, which makes it difficult for them to spot danger. Consequently, they have developed what to us might seem to be a rather daft response. Any time they spot anything that looks remotely like danger, they will charge at it, even if it means they end up crashing into trees or boulders. Despite their bulky size, rhinos are amazingly quick, charging at speeds of up to 45 kilometres per hour (28 mph), which is marginally faster than even the top speed of Usain Bolt.

Why do ostriches eat stones?

Ostriches are often thought to be stupid, and anyone witnessing one picking up and swallowing mouthfuls of grit and stones might think this reputation well deserved. However, ostriches are perhaps not quite as stupid as they look, as this collection of gravel actually serves a crucial purpose. Incidentally, the other reason ostriches are thought stupid – that they stick their heads in the sand – is simply untrue.

One of the defining features of birds is that they have a beak, rather than a mouth full of teeth. Beaks are light, powerful and aerodynamic, but they are no good for chewing, and a bird's diet often does need to be chewed. The solution to this conundrum is that the chewing takes place not in the bird's mouth, but deep inside its stomach, in a second chamber called the gizzard. A gizzard looks like a flat, round purse, with thick, ridged walls, which contract rhythmically to grind the bird's food and break it down, with the help of digestive juices produced by the stomach's first chamber.

In fact, all birds have a gizzard, but birds that live on seeds need extra abrasive power to break down the seeds' resilient coatings and shells, so they fill their gizzard with grit. Grit works well, as it weighs less than a mouthful of teeth, and its location in the stomach is more aerodynamic and better balanced for flight. Nonetheless, the extra weight is still a consideration, so some birds get rid of their grit at certain times of the year, when their diet switches to insects. Some birds, on the other hand, spend very little time in the air, and so are less troubled by the question of weight. Consequently, larger birds such as turkeys, chickens and ostriches, which tend not to spend much time in the air, have large gizzards, containing a lot of grit.

Are elephants really scared of mice?

It's an amusing idea, but in fact there is no evidence for the belief that elephants are scared of mice. Elephants have very poor eyesight, so even if a mouse were running around its feet, the odds are that an elephant wouldn't even notice it. Elephants rely to a large degree on their excellent sense of smell, but mice simply don't have a strong enough smell to gain an elephant's attention. Like most animals, elephants are only afraid of their predators, which in the case of elephants is a small group consisting of big cats such as lions and tigers, and of course humans.

So where did this myth come from? It goes back at least as far as the ancient Greeks, who told a fable about a mouse that crawled up an elephant's trunk, and drove it insane. There is also another similar fable, a bit like the story of the old woman who swallowed a fly. In this story, a village becomes overrun by mice. The villagers decide to bring in cats to get rid of the mice, but soon find they have a cat problem. They bring in dogs to deal with the cats, and then bulls to deal with the dogs, then finally elephants to deal with the bulls. Eventually, they bring in mice to scare away the elephants, returning the village to its original state.

Which are cleverer: dogs or cats?

Comparing the intelligence of different types of animal is arguably an impossible task, particularly when their habits and lifestyles are as different as those of dogs and cats. After all, there are considerable, possibly insurmountable, difficulties in trying to measure and compare the intelligence of human beings, and we all belong to the same species, and communicate with one another.

Nonetheless, there are certain ways of approaching the question that might be helpful. One way to measure intelligence might be to consider the weight of the animal's brain in relation to its size, which is known as the encephalisation quotient or EQ. Among mammals above a certain size, human beings have the highest brain-to-weight ratio, and this reflects our elevated position as the most intelligent of the animals. A human's brain makes up around

2.1 per cent of his or her body weight. A small dog's brain makes up on average around 0.65 per cent of its weight, while the brain of the domestic cat comprises only 0.60 per cent of its weight. So, does this mean dogs are smarter? Sadly not. For one thing, the size of the dog seems to make an enormous difference: the corresponding figure for large dogs is that their brains make up on average just 0.38 per cent of their body weight.

Another measure of intelligence is the degree to which an animal can learn and be trained. In this respect, dogs would seem to be vastly superior. Like us, dogs are social creatures, that derive significant evolutionary benefits from working collaboratively. Living in packs means that dogs have to be able to pick up cues from one another, and take instructions. Cats on the other hand are solitary hunters, who have consequently never needed to learn these skills. As a result, cats are very difficult to train.

Yet another measure of intelligence is an animal's ability to solve simple problems, and a recent study suggests that in this respect too dogs have the upper hand. Researchers set up a simple 'string test', in which pulling the string would release a treat of fish or biscuits. When presented with a single string, with a reward at the end, cats and dogs both managed to work out how to solve the problem. However, when given a choice between two parallel strings, none of the cats learned to consistently choose the one that delivered the reward, whereas the dogs did learn this. The third stage of the test presented the animals with crossed strings, complicating the problem further, and neither the cats nor the dogs succeeded in consistently working this out.

In 1998, researchers at Oregon State University conducted a survey of students, faculty members and staff from various departments, in which they asked the respondents various questions about how intelligent they thought different types of animal were. In response to some of the questions, such as whether or not animals have the ability to think, there was a wide range of contrasting views. However, when asked to rank various animals in order of intelligence, there was a high degree of conformity in the responses given. In order from highest intelligence to lowest, the respondents ranked the animals thus: dog, cat, pig, horse, cow, sheep, chicken and turkey.

Do any animals mourn?

The ability to feel sorrow at the death of a friend or loved one would seem to offer no obvious evolutionary advantage, so it is somewhat surprising to find that a number of animals do seem to mourn or grieve their dead. Elephants have been long believed to have elaborate mourning practices. Elephants have large brains and, in some respects, display considerable intelligence. For one thing, they are one of the very few animals, along with dolphins and some primates, who can recognise their own reflection in a mirror. A recent study confirmed that elephants do pay particular attention to the bones and skulls of other elephants. Elephants will visit the site of elephants' bones, and spend time touching and stroking the bones with their trunk and feet.

There is also some evidence that primates can feel grief. Baboons have been observed seeking the comfort of friends when a close family member dies, with a corresponding increase in their stress levels. The primatologist Jane Goodall also believes that primates can grieve. She describes a young chimpanzee called Flint, who, she believes, had died from grief after the death of his mother. Gorillas are even said to hold wakes for the death of a high-ranking companion.

Shingleback lizards also seem to respond to the death of a loved one. When a young male is ready to mate, he will travel long distances in search of a partner. When he finds a receptive female, he will follow her, attracted by her pheromone-laden scent. The pair may stay together for six to eight weeks before separating, with the male playing no part in raising the young. However, the following spring, he will once again seek out the same partner, and the couple may stay together in this intermittent way for twenty years. If one of the pair dies, its partner may be seen standing over the body, gently licking it, as if grieving the death of its spouse.

CHAPTER FIVE

Filthy fauna

Which frog coughs up its entire stomach?

When they need to vomit, some frogs have an incredible technique. Instead of simply expelling the stomach's contents, as we do, they cough up their entire stomach, and then carefully rinse it out with their right hand, before pushing it back inside and swallowing it. And why do they always rinse it with their right hand, rather than their left? Apparently, it is because the tissues that hold the stomach in place are shorter on the right-hand side, which means that, when the frog expels its stomach, it always hangs to the right, where it can be washed only by the right hand.

Why does the Australian rainbow pitta decorate its nest with wallaby poo?

The rainbow pitta is an attractive and colourful Australian bird, which is known as the 'jewel of the forest'. It is similar in size and shape to a thrush, reaching about 20 centimetres (8 inches) in length. It has a velvet black head and breast, with green upper parts, and an electric-blue patch on its wing. The pitta is found in the rainforests, mangroves and eucalyptus forests of northern Australia, where it lives on a diet of snails, worms and insects.

Rainbow pittas are shy, sensitive birds, which are difficult to observe. They breed seasonally, to coincide with the onset of the rainy season, between October and March. They usually build their nests in trees, but will also nest on clumps of bamboo, thickets, tree stumps, or even on the ground. Their nests are fairly sloppy constructions, made of twigs and leaves, in the shape of a rugby ball. The interior of the nest is lined with fine leaves, and is reached via an entrance hole in the side of the dome. Next to this entrance, the rainbow pitta will often lay a kind of doormat, which it makes out of wallaby poo.

As you can imagine, a doormat made of poo in a tropical climate can get a bit stinky, but the bird doesn't seem to mind. In fact, the pong seems to be the point. In the forests where the rainbow pitta is found, brown tree snakes pose a significant threat. These snakes will eat the bird's eggs if they find the nest, and for this they rely on their powerful sense of smell, as it seems that the rainbow pitta's (undecorated) nest has a distinctive odour. For this reason, the birds have developed the habit of decorating their nest with pungent wallaby poo, which they collect assiduously from the forest floor, as a kind of olfactory camouflage, to fool their slithering predators.

Which animal loves to collect pellets of owl vomit?

Bizarrely, the answer is human beings. Let's look at why owls produce these pellets in the first place. Owls are birds of prey, whose diet includes small mammals such as moles, rats, mice and voles, as well as insects and small birds. Owls have no teeth to chew with, so they swallow their prey whole, head first. The owl's digestive juices will then strip the meat from the bones, macerating it using the gizzard's muscular walls. Later, the owl will vomit up all the inedible parts of its meal, which by now will have been rolled

into a pellet, comprising some combination of fur, teeth, claws, feathers and bones. This is known as an 'owl pellet'.

In fact, many birds of prey produce similar pellets, but owl pellets' are particularly easy to find, because they are usually found beneath a favoured spot for feeding or roosting. These pellets may then get used in a number of ways. They can become food or a home for various types of insect, including carpet beetles. Clothes moths use them as a nursery, and lay their eggs inside the pellet. As the clothes moth larvae develop, they make their cocoons inside the pellet, using the leftover fur.

Owl pellets are also quite useful for humans, as we like to collect them for their scientific value. Because owls eat their prey whole, their pellets contain the entire skeletons of whatever animals they have eaten. An average pellet will contain the skeletons of three animals, and these can be rearranged and put together again, producing a pristine model. Consequently, these pellets can be used as a fascinating and stimulating way to teach children about science, birds and local wildlife.

The other reason we collect owl pellets is to keep track of what the owls are eating, and to measure the local populations of small animals. Obviously, keeping track of how many mice or voles there are in a given area is a very difficult task, so regular studies of owl pellets provide a useful and consistent guide. However, owl pellets can carry viruses and bacteria from rodents, so, if you are tempted to collect or dissect one, it's a good idea to sterilise it first by heating it in a microwave.

Which bird kills its enemies by throwing up on them?

The fulmar is a large seabird that looks a lot like a seagull. The name 'fulmar' means 'foul gull', and the name is well deserved, because the fulmar's main mode of defence is to vomit a disgusting yellow oil over its enemies. This vomit is not only unpleasant and smelly, it is also potentially lethal. Most of the fulmar's predators are birds of prey, including skuas, ospreys and sea eagles. The fulmar's vomit sticks to their feathers, making them unable to fly. It can even cause them to drown.

In fulmar families, both parents go hunting at sea, for up to twenty hours at a time, which means their nests are left undefended. The chicks are obviously not strong enough to defend themselves against birds of prey in a conventional way, so as soon as they are hatched, fulmar chicks have this amazing ability to vomit oil, and to aim it with precision. At just four days old, they can puke as far as half a metre, while older chicks can spew three times as far. When they are born, the chicks even instinctively vomit at their parents, until they learn to recognise them as family.

Why are penguins such powerful pooers?

Some people get all the best jobs. A group of European scientists recently conducted a study of penguin faeces, which found that the birds could expel their poo with a force of up to 60 kilopascals (a pascal is a unit of pressure) – four times greater than a human being's equivalent poo power. Further, the penguins could expel their poo to a distance of 40 centimetres (16 inches). It seems that the reason the penguin has developed this unusual talent is to avoid soiling its feathers or its nest. For this unusual research, the scientists in question were awarded an Ig Nobel prize, which is a light-hearted science prize designed to honour scientific achievements that 'make people laugh – then think'.

However, penguins are not the only power pooers out there. Kingfishers and hornbills will back up to the entrance of their waterside treehole to expel a stream directly into the river, which will usually be powerful enough to avoid leaving any streak or mark on the tree or the riverbank. The reason for this is to avoid detection by predators – if their tree were marked with faeces, their hole would be easily discovered. One reason why birds are able to develop such a gift is that they produce their urine and faeces in one single stream, making it runnier than the excrement of mammals. This technique not only protects the birds from detection by predators, it also keeps their nests clean, limiting the risk of infection and disease.

Which bird disguises itself as cow dung?

The nacunda nighthawk lives out on the open plains of Brazil. It is a type of nightjar, which spends most of its days resting on the ground. There are no trees or bushes in which to hide from predators, so the bird would seem to be completely exposed, but it has developed a cunning form of camouflage. It crouches, and in doing so it resembles a pile of unappetising cow dung.

The amazing thing about this is that cows are a fairly recent addition to the wildlife of Brazil. There were no cows in Brazil until just a few centuries ago, when they were introduced by European explorers. And there are no other large grazing mammals on the plains of Brazil, which might produce something similar to cow poo. This raises a fascinating question: how did the nacunda nighthawk evolve to resemble a pile of cow poo, if there were no cows around to produce poo in the first place? It could not have evolved this talent in just a few centuries.

Scientists do have a theory to explain this strange conundrum. Although there are no other large grazing mammals on the plains today, once upon a time, there were. Around a thousand years ago, these grasslands were the home of giant sloths and great arma-dillos, which were the size of today's cows. These creatures have been extinct for centuries, but the fact of their existence raises the amazing possibility that the nacunda nighthawk's camouflage may actually be providing us with an accurate picture of what their excrement looked like, all those centuries ago.

Why do vultures poo on themselves?

Staying cool is a difficult art to master. The only class of animals that have sweat glands are the mammals, and even then only some mammals have sweat glands. Dogs, cats and rodents, for example, have lost most or all of their sweat glands. Mammals that lack sweat glands generally cool down by flushing or panting. Birds, on the other hand, tend to cool themselves by raising their down feathers, to increase air flow to the skin. They also take baths, and pant.

However, some birds, including vultures, also do something fairly disgusting called urohydrosis, which means they urinate and defecate down their legs. Birds have a single genital opening called a cloaca, which means that their waste products all come out together. This is why bird poo is often so runny, because it also contains the bird's urine. It may sounds gross, but this habit probably helps to keep the birds clean, in a perverse way. Bird poo contains uric acid, which is an antiseptic. Defecating down its own legs may therefore help keep a vulture free from germs after it has walked through a rotting carcass.

Some cranes and storks approach the problem of temperature management in a slightly different way. Their chicks are reared on stick platforms in tropical climates, where the heat of the sun can be very damaging. The chicks are not yet able to fend for themselves, and so, as a result, it falls to the birds' parents to keep them cool somehow. They do this by collecting stomachfuls of water, and vomiting over their young, giving them a refreshing shower. Herons solve this problem in an arguably even more unpleasant way: they simply poo over their young.

Are cows' farts a major cause of climate change?

It is true that cows' farts produce carbon dioxide, and that too much carbon dioxide in the atmosphere is one of the most significant factors responsible for the greenhouse effect, leading to global warming. However, the amount of carbon dioxide produced by cows is actually relatively small. In fact, the problem isn't cows' farts, but rather their burps.

Cows, sheep and other ruminants live on a diet of grass,

which is very difficult to break down, but so low in nutrition that any large animal seeking to subsist on it needs to extract as much goodness as possible. Ruminants achieve this by chewing and regurgitating their food over and over again, using bacteria in their stomachs to digest it. This process produces a gas called methane, which is another greenhouse gas, and one that is far more damaging to the environment than carbon dioxide (CO_2). There is far less methane in the atmosphere than CO_2 – just two parts per million, compared with 384 parts per million of CO_2 – but it absorbs 25 times more heat than CO_2, which means its total impact on global warming is about a third that of all the carbon dioxide.

A single cow burps up around 80–110 kilograms of methane each year. Altogether, there are about 1.2 billion sheep, cows, goats and other ruminants on the planet, which collectively produce around 80 million tonnes of methane a year. This is a significant amount, around 12 per cent of the global total, but it is dwarfed by other sources of methane such as plants, waste dumps, termites, bacteria, and sewerage works.

So what's the solution? We can hardly ask the cows to stop burping. Well, a number of approaches have been suggested. Scientists in Aberdeen have developed a feed additive that they think may decrease cattle methane production by as much 70 per cent. Researchers in Aberystwyth are looking into a new form of rye grass with a higher sugar content; the theory being that sugar will increase the effectiveness of the cow's digestive system, thus reducing the methane produced by bacteria.

One other proposal is that people should start eating a different type of meat: specifically, kangaroo meat. As bizarre as it may sound, kangaroo meat offers many potential benefits. Kangaroos emit far less greenhouse gas than cattle – a kangaroo produces around a third of the methane of a ruminant such as a cow or a sheep. Kangaroo meat is high in protein, and low in fat. It also contains a high concentration of conjugated linoleic acid (CLA), which has been found to have anti-cancer properties, as well as reducing body fat. Australians already eat kangaroo; if you go to an Aussie supermarket, you will find kangaroo steaks, kangaroo burgers, and even 'kanga bangas', which are (in case you haven't worked it out already) kangaroo sausages!

How does the Gila monster keep cool?

The Gila monster is a large, venomous lizard that's found in the south-western United States and northern Mexico. It's a slow, cumbersome creature, which can reach around 60 centimetres (2 feet) in length. It lives in the desert, where the temperature frequently reaches 40 degrees Celsius (104 degrees Fahrenheit). Many species of lizard live in similarly hot climates, and most of them use a number of techniques for keeping cool. They stay in the shade, they minimise their points of contact with the hot ground, and they open their mouths, like dogs panting.

However, the Gila monster has a rather different technique for keeping cool. Instead of opening its mouth, it opens its anus, or rather, its cloaca. Many lizards, amphibians and birds have a cloaca, which is a single orifice used for urinating, defecating, copulation and giving birth. By opening its cloaca, the Gila monster cools itself by shedding moisture into the atmosphere.

But why doesn't it just open its mouth, like other lizards? The answer isn't entirely clear, but one possible explanation is that the Gila monster relies on its venom for hunting, whereas most lizards are not venomous. The Gila monster's venom is released straight into its mouth like saliva, so it's possible that cooling itself by opening its mouth would compromise either its ability to produce this venom, or the quality of the venom.

Which insect lives on mucus from the inside of a cow's nostrils?

This is the rather unpleasant diet of the face fly, or *Musca autumnalis*. To the untrained eye, this insect looks exactly like a housefly, but entomologists can tell the difference, because the eyes of the two species are of slightly different shapes, and their abdomens are a slightly different colour. Face flies are found throughout most of North America, Europe and Asia, and are a major pest for cattle and horses.

Face flies hibernate over the winter, and then emerge in the spring. The females lay their eggs in fresh manure, and these eggs usually hatch within twenty-four hours. The maggots then metamorphose through a number of stages, while feeding on the manure, before moving to an area of nearby soil for the final stage of their development. Depending on the local temperature, an adult fly will emerge in about two to three weeks.

Adult face flies live and feed on cattle, dining mainly on the animal's facial secretions, including tears, nasal mucus, sweat and saliva. They have abrasive, spongy mouthparts, which soak up these protein-rich secretions, and also cause the animal's eyes to produce more tears, which in turn attract more face flies. They are not considered to be blood feeders, because their mouthparts are not able to pierce the host's skin, but given the chance they will feed on wounds opened up by other blood-feeding flies.

Face flies are usually the most numerous flies found on cattle, and they can be irritating enough to interfere with the animal's ability to graze. They can also transmit the bacteria that cause eyeworm and pinkeye in cattle. Because they are usually found around the eyes and nose, they are very difficult to treat with insecticides.

However, we should not feel too smug about the burdens tolerated by our slow-witted, four-legged friends, because we humans suffer from a very similar pest. The eye gnat is a type of tiny fly, around 2 millimetres in length, which is found in many hot climates, including the southern USA. In the summer, eye gnats congregate around our eyes and nose, and sup on the moisture, causing considerable annoyance.

Which type of ant loves hospitals?

There is a type of ant called the pharaoh ant, which is commonly found in hospitals. It is one of the smaller species of ant, with workers measuring just 2 millimetres long. These yellow-brown ants form large colonies, and favour warm, indoor conditions, because they need a warm temperature in which to breed. As a result, they are often found in centrally heated buildings such as hospitals, nursing homes, hotels, restaurants, and apartment blocks.

They particularly thrive in hospitals, because they like to eat a diet rich in protein, and so they feast on bloody bandages, dressings, IV solutions, and surgical wounds. They are trail-making ants, who can communicate information about new sources of food and water to one another, which helps the population to spread. Because they seek out sources of water, they will often find their way to toilets, drains and bedpans, which makes them a serious health risk, as they are capable of transmitting diseases, infecting foodstuffs, and contaminating sterile materials.

Pharaoh ants are a nuisance because they spread easily, and they are very difficult to get rid of. Unlike most types of ant, pharaoh ant colonies can contain a number of queens, as many as two hundred in some cases. Colonies spread by 'budding', which means that a group of queens and workers will break away from the main colony and set up a nearby nest. Pharaoh ants are also unusual in that they don't differentiate between nestmates and ants from 'rival' nests, so there is no hostility between nearby colonies.

Consequently, pharaoh ant infestations are extremely difficult to get rid of, as there will usually be lots of nesting sites, rather than just one. Pharaoh ants can colonise a large apartment block in just a few months. Colonies can also contract in size while pest-control measures are taken, before regrouping and expanding once the threat has passed.

How do lobsters grow?

Lobsters are invertebrates, which have a hard protective exoskeleton. An exoskeleton is an external skeleton, in contrast to the internal skeleton that we have, which is called an endoskeleton. One of the problems with an exoskeleton is that it limits a creature's growth, because the exoskeleton itself is rigid, and cannot grow. Lobsters can live for a hundred years, and they grow substantially throughout their lives. So how do they manage to grow, if their shell can't?

The answer is that they regularly shed their shell, and replace it with a new one. Doing so is a dramatic and extremely dangerous procedure. A lobster's exoskeleton includes its teeth, which are found inside its stomach. This means that, to replace its shell, a lobster has to rip out the lining of its own throat, stomach and anus. This is as perilous and unpleasant as it sounds, and many lobsters die in the process.

Why are pigs so dirty?

Actually, pigs are unjustly maligned. When we want to describe a person as being dirty, greedy, stupid, lazy, stubborn, sweaty, or rude, we will often compare them to a pig, but in fact all of these clichés about pigs are quite untrue. Despite their reputation, pigs are intelligent creatures, with modest appetites, who are not nearly as dirty as they may appear.

Many animals will overeat given the chance, including horses, sheep and ourselves, but pigs rarely do. It is true that they eat a wide range of foods, but this is not to say that they lack discernment. On the contrary, they have three times as many taste buds as human beings, and they particularly dislike certain foods such as lemon rind and raw onions (and who can blame them?). Pigs are also surprisingly clean animals. They are the only farm animals who make a separate sleeping area for themselves, and they keep it fastidiously clean. They also use a separate latrine area, to avoid disease and infection. Rather than sweating like pigs, in fact they don't sweat at all, as they don't have any sweat glands. This is why they wallow in mud, to keep cool, and avoid sunburn.

They are also surprisingly intelligent. Pigs can be trained, and make excellent pets. The American actor George Clooney was particularly attached to his Vietnamese potbellied pig, Max, with whom he even sometimes shared his bed. Pigs can be housetrained, and taught to fetch and heel, just like dogs. In studies, pigs have even learned to play video games, manipulating the joystick with their snouts, which is something that even chimpanzees struggle to learn.

Why is it that people get fleas, but apes don't?

Fleas are parasites that live by feeding on the blood of birds and mammals. There are a number of different species of flea, which feed on different host animals, and are consequently known by names such as cat flea, dog flea, northern rat flea, Oriental rat flea and human flea. However, there is no ape flea, even though one would imagine that apes must surely be at least as dirty as we are. So how is it that we get fleas, but apes don't?

The simple answer is that human beings provide fleas with a home in which to live, whereas apes don't. It is a common misconception that fleas live on their hosts, but actually this is true of only a few types of flea, which attach themselves to their host's hair or feathers. Most fleas live in the host's nest or bedding, and jump on board only when they are hungry. This is why the only mammals that fleas tend to infest are those that maintain a regular, warm burrow or den, such as cats, dogs, rabbits, rats, bats and humans. Apes, on the other hand, live in the wild, and do not keep a regular nest or den. Consequently, there is nowhere for a flea to set up home.

However, this does raise an interesting question. Since we are evolved from apes, and apes do not get fleas, where did our fleas come from? The answer seems to be that we caught our fleas from badgers or pigs, probably when we began to make our first primitive homes. In fact, although the flea which infests us is known as the human flea, it is not exclusive to us, as it also continues to infest pigs and badgers, as well as dogs, cats, rats and other creatures.

Why do birds rub ants into their wings?

Most animals that inadvertently disturb a wood ants' nest soon come to regret it, as the worker ants swarm out in an angry mob. These ants do not sting: instead, they fight off intruders by squirting jets of formic acid into the air, from glands at the end of their abdomen. This is enough to repel most creatures, but some birds actively seek out this treatment, deliberately flying down to land on ants' nests, and provoking them to squirt.

Jays, starlings and crows all enjoy sitting on ants' nests, in a process called 'anting'. As the angry ants swarm over them, the birds will erect their feathers, letting the ants discharge acid into every crevice. Some even pick up ants in their beaks, and rub them over their feathers, as if squeezing out as much acid as they can get. The reason they do this is that the acid cleans the birds' feathers, and rids them of any fleas, lice, or other skin parasites they might have picked up. However, anting does not seem to be a purely functional chore. Many birds seem to actively enjoy it, cocking their heads back and closing their eyes, as if thrilled by the invigorating sting of the formic acid.

Birds are not the only creatures that enjoy the attentions of a raging ant swarm. Tortoises are burdened with cumbersome shells, which are very difficult to clean, making it impossible for the tortoise to remove any ticks or parasites that may have climbed on board. The North American wood tortoise uses ants to help keep it clean. It will simply walk into the ants' nest and sit still, while the insects swarm all over it, squirting anti-microbial acid, and killing any parasites they may come across.

How do hedgehogs anoint themselves?

Surprisingly perhaps, given their prickly appearance, hedgehogs are regarded as one the animal kingdom's cutest creatures. However, they have one very disgusting habit. A hedgehog will contort its body, and spit foaming saliva all over its own back. It does this after chewing on the toxic skin of a toad, which produces a poisonous mousse, with which the hedgehog covers its spines. It's not clear why it does this, but presumably the foam is useful for deterring predators.

This habit may also help to explain how hedgehogs have developed such incredible immunity to poison. Hedgehogs can survive a bite from an adder which would kill a guinea pig in five minutes. Also, it takes more chloroform to knock out a hedgehog than any other creature of a similar size.

Why are pigs so ugly?

Having defended pigs a few pages back, we should now admit that some species of pig are fantastically ugly. It's not clear why, but many species of pig have evolved weird tusks, moustaches, snouts and other strange facial features. A number of pigs have special teeth that have grown into tusks, including the warthog, wild boar, giant forest hog, and the European pig. Some of these tusks have grown to an enormous size, and are used for a variety of functions. Wild boars use them for digging up roots and truffles, and other pigs use them when they fight one another. Since these tusks are usually bigger in males than females, they may also be used for sexual display.

Other pigs are stranger still. The African red river hog has a tremendous moustache. The warthog has, as well as its tusks, two large warts under its eyes, which serve to protect the eyes from the tusks of rival males when they fight. However, the weirdest-looking pig is probably a rare species called the babirusa, which is found only on the Indonesian island of Sulawesi. This pig has two fairly routine tusks growing from its lower jaw. However, it also grows a third tusk from its upper jaw, which grows right through the flesh of its snout, and curves backwards towards its forehead, as if trying to impale its owner.

How does the brown hyena communicate?

There are few creatures whose anal secretions could be described as elegant and sophisticated, but the brown hyena is one of them. In the Kalahari desert, brown hyenas are constantly marking their territory, and they do this by a complex system of smelly deposits. They live in clans of about a dozen, and travel long distances looking for food, which for the brown hyena consists of carrion, and sometimes small mammals. Every few minutes, the hyena will 'mark', by straddling a clump of grass, and smearing it with oil from its anal gland.

Other mammals mark their territory in a similar way, including civets, but the hyena's system is unusually sophisticated. The brown hyena simultaneously produces two distinct types of anal secretion: a white paste, which forms a small bead on the grass stem; and an even smaller blob of black oil, which sticks just above it. These two markers serve very different functions. The white bead is a sign of ownership, warning hyenas of other clans that this territory is taken. This bead retains its powerful smell for several weeks. The black bead, on the other hand, is intended as a message for other members of the hyena's own clan. It loses its smell very quickly, and vanishes within a few hours. The strength of this bead's smell therefore communicates to any passing hyena how recently this territory was patrolled, and therefore whether or not it is likely to offer much food. In any single clan's territory, there may be up to fifteen thousand of these whiffy signposts, and they are frequently updated.

How do rhinos mark their territory?

With poo, and lots of it! Some animals eat their dung, others bury it, others hide it, or present it to their partner as a gift. But rhinos put it on display, in enormous piles more than a metre wide. The rhino uses these to mark the boundaries of its territory, and may have as many as 30 piles dotted around, and he will try to visit each of them every day.

The piles serve two useful purposes. First they notify rival rhinos that this territory is taken, warning them not to trespass. Second they help the owner of the territory to locate himself. Rhinos have very poor eyesight, which makes it difficult for them to recognise landmarks. However, their sense of smell is excellent, so these dung piles serve as helpful olfactory signposts.

Why do sloths turn green?

Sloths are medium-sized mammals, usually about half a metre (about 20 inches) long, who live in the treetops in the rainforests of Central and South America. The local tribes in Ecuador refer to sloths using three rather unkind names: *rittor*, *rit*, and *ridette*, which derive from the local words for 'sleep', 'eat', and 'dirty'. It's true that sloths do little more than eat and sleep, and they spend their lives hanging upside down from the branches of the trees in which they live. This is because their diet of leaves is very low in nutrients, so they have to expend as little energy as possible. Consequently, sloths have a much lower body temperature and metabolic rate than other mammals of a similar size.

The third accusation, that sloths are dirty, is sadly also true. A sloth's fur is a kind of yellowy-brown when the sloth is young, but as it gets older, its fur gradually turns green. This green colour comes from a kind of algae that grows on the sloth's fur. Turning green is useful for the sloths, since it helps to camouflage them in the treetops, making it harder for eagles to see them – eagles are the sloth's only predator. The algae also makes a useful snack, because it contains lots of beneficial nutrients, so the sloths will frequently be seen snacking on lumps from their fur.

Which bird mugs other birds for their vomit?

The magnificent frigate bird is found around the coast of Australia and the Pacific Islands. The 'magnificent' in its name refers to its size – the bird's wingspan is an enormous two metres (6.5 feet), but it could also describe the frigate bird's aerial prowess. The frigate bird is an amazing acrobat that can skim the surface of the sea and snatch fish near the surface using its hooked beak.

However, it also has another way of hunting, which we might struggle to consider magnificent: it mugs other birds in flight, to steal their vomit. The frigate bird can tell when another bird is flying home after a successful fishing mission. It will attack this bird in flight, perhaps tugging on its tail feathers. The victim, often a booby, will be knocked off balance, and throw up its catch. The frigate bird then swoops into a dive and catches the regurgitated fish before it hits the water.

In Mexico, the aplomado falcon is another aerial pirate. Like the frigate bird, it is quite capable of catching its own prey, but studies have found that its odds of success are greater if it simply steals from other birds. Researchers found that the falcon's piracy attempts were successful 82 per cent of the time, whereas actually trying to hunt for itself produced results only 38 per cent of the time.

Why do dogs eat poo?

Pet owners often report that their dogs will not stop eating poo, no matter how well they're fed and cared for, but as yet there's no clear consensus as to why they do this, although there are many theories. Some say the dog may be lacking certain nutrients. Others suggest that the dog may be under stress, or seeking attention from its owner. Another theory is that the dog is trying to hide the scent of its poo, to avoid attracting predators. Yet another theory holds that because most domestic dogs will have been punished for defecating at some point, this may be their attempt to hide the evidence, and thus avoid displeasing their owner.

There may be no conclusive answer as yet, but we do know that eating poo is not confined to dogs. A great

number of animal species regularly eat their own poo, including rabbits, Japanese hares, northern pika, sportive lemurs, koalas, possums, chinchillas, European beavers, guinea pigs and Norway lemmings. This suggests that at least some of these species derive some useful benefit from it.

Rabbits routinely eat their own leavings, and for them it seems to be simply one stage of the digestive process. A rabbit's diet consists of grass, leaves and other plant matter. This is a diet that is low in nutrients, and difficult to digest. To ensure that they are getting as much energy and nutrition out of their food as possible, rabbits eat their poo as soon as it emerges from their anus. This lets the rabbit's stomach give the food a second digestive processing. The round dry pellets that you see in a rabbit warren are what's left after the rabbit has digested its food twice.

Other animals are believed to eat their poo for rather different reasons. Many bird species are particularly careful about hiding their poo, for fear of alerting predators to the location of their nest. In the first few days of their life, the chicks of many species produce faeces enclosed in a gelatinous sac. Their parents will swallow this, and some seem to actually enjoy eating it, which suggests that the poo may retain some nutritional value that the chick's undeveloped stomach was unable to process. The parent birds even encourage the chicks to poo, poking their anus after feeding, until the chick produces a little white sac of excrement. As the chick gets older, the parent bird will stop eating its faeces, and instead carry it away to be dumped.

Why do frogs eat their own skin?

Frogs have soft, delicate skin, which wears away quickly, and has to be frequently replaced. Many frogs shed their skin as often as once a week. The process begins with a lot of twisting, bending and stretching, to loosen the old skin. The outer layer becomes separated from the new skin growing underneath, and begins to split. The frog will scratch at its skin, loosening the outer layer with its forelegs, as if pulling off a scab; in fact, it may well itch and annoy the frog, just like a scab. At some point, the frog will be able to get part of the skin in its mouth, and then it will gradually pull the whole thing into its mouth, still loosening it with its legs, until the whole skin has been swallowed. Disgusting though this may sound, growing a new skin takes a lot of energy and nutrients, and so this way the frog gets to recycle as much of this as possible. So you see, it's true: frogs really are green!

Which creature eats with its eyes?

It's not a trick question. Frogs and toads really do use their eyes to eat with. So, how does it work? Well, they don't use their eyes as a mouth. They don't chew with them, or ingest food through them. Instead, they use their eyes to push their food down into their stomach when they swallow. When a frog eats a tasty morsel, such as a small cricket, it will close its eyes, and retract its eyeballs into its body. These push into the frog's pharynx, against the cricket, and repeated pushes gradually force the food down to the back of the frog's oesophagus.

How is urban living having a negative effect on the youth of Florida?

In the case of scrub-jays, urban convenience and fast food are playing havoc with the health of the species' young. The people of Florida are bird lovers, who like to encourage the wonderful variety of birds in their state to spend time in their gardens. As you would imagine, these well-meaning locals build birdhouses and bird feeders, and leave out tasty treats of nuts and seeds for their colourful visitors.

However, the timing of the scrub-jays' mating season is triggered by an increase in the amount of available food, which traditionally could only have meant that spring had arrived. However, the intervention of well-meaning humans, before the dawn of spring, can create an artificial abundance of food, causing the city's birds to breed earlier, and to lay more eggs, than their country cousins.

So why is this a problem? Food is abundant, so why shouldn't they breed earlier? The problem is that the diet of nuts, seeds and other plant-based foods provided by humans, while more than adequate for an adult scrub-jay's needs, does not suit the young hatchlings, who require foods rich in protein, such as insect larvae and grubs, to help them to grow quickly. However, these grubs and larvae don't appear until later in the year, which means the young scrub-jays suffer from malnutrition, which sadly will stunt their growth, and may even kill them.

CHAPTER SIX

Sexy species

What is 'penis fencing'?

The vast majority of worm species are hermaphrodites, which means that they have both male and female sexual organs. One of these species, a flatworm called *Pseudoceros bifurcens*, performs a bizarre mating ritual, which is best described as penis fencing. When two of the worms meet, they fence, using their pointy, dagger-like penises. The first one to inject the other with sperm is the winner, as 'he' gets to be the male. His sperm gets absorbed into the loser's skin, and 'she' becomes the female. The reason why both worms compete to take the male role is that giving birth takes up a considerable amount of the mother's energy, nutrition and other resources, so it is preferable, from a flatworm's point of view, to be the father. However, there do exist other types of hermaphroditic creatures that compete to be inseminated, and to take the female role.

How do slugs have sex?

Slugs have a range of fascinating and disgusting ways of pairing up and reproducing. Like worms, slugs are also hermaphrodites. Each of them has two pairs of tentacles on its head. One pair is longer than the other, with an eye on each tip. The shorter pair can smell another slug's chemical pheromones. When a slug that is looking for a mate finds a slimy trail, it can smell whether or not the slug that left it was in the mood for romance. If so, it will start to chase this slug, waving its tentacles frantically, although obviously this all takes place much more slowly than this description probably suggests. The first slug will now start to crawl in a circle, while being pursued by the second slug. This chase goes on for as long as an hour, with the circle gradually getting smaller, until finally they meet in the middle; side by side and head to tail, like a slimy yin and yang. Now, at last, each of them will extrude its penis, and inseminate the other. They both slither away pregnant.

The courtship of a type of creature called the leopard slug is even more elaborate. In this species, the slug being chased will seek out an overhanging surface, such as a tree branch, where the two will continue their circling. They then entwine their bodies around one another, before diving off the branch, in a slow-motion descent, as they twist around on a rope of slime, like a pair of very slow, very gooey bungee jumpers. Once they have fallen about a foot, they will stop their descent, and entwine their penises around each other. As the slugs tighten their coils around each other, their penises suddenly open up like an umbrella, and they exchange sperm. They then go their separate ways, completely unaware of quite how weird the thing that they just did was!

Yet another slug has an even more extraordinary way of having sex. The banana slug is found in the western USA, and is much larger than any slug found in Europe, reaching lengths of up to 25 centimetres (10 inches). Like the other slugs we've described, it will begin a circling courtship dance. During this, however, the slugs will attack each other, biting each other's flanks, tearing out lumps of flesh. The strangeness doesn't end there. In between attacking each other, they bash their own foreparts against the ground, as well as pulling out their penises and waving them at each other. Amazingly, this odd behaviour may continue for as long as twelve hours. Eventually, though, they decide that the foreplay is over, and exchange sperm. With the formalities out of the way, one of the partners will now usually bite off the other's penis and eat it.

Why does the female praying mantis bite off her partner's head during sex?

Praying mantises are an order of large insects, usually around 8–12 centimetres (3–5 inches) long, which are found in most temperate and tropical parts of the world. They are vicious predators, capable of killing animals much bigger

than themselves, including lizards, frogs and small birds. Mantises hold their forelegs up in front of their head, as if praying, which is the reason for their unusual name.

Perhaps the most notable thing about praying mantises is their amazing reproductive habits. During sex, the female will reach around and bite the male's head clean off. Incredibly, even after being decapitated, the male will continue to thrust for an hour or more, and his movements may even become more vigorous. As a result, scientists have long believed that this cannibalistic behaviour may actually help reproduction, by prolonging the mating process and increasing the odds of fertilisation. Also, when the female then eats the rest of her partner's body, this provides her with a healthy meal full of vital nutrients, which help with the development of her eggs.

However, there is growing doubt about this explanation. A number of recent studies have attempted to observe praying mantises mating in more natural conditions, without the obvious presence of human observers or harsh laboratory lighting. The results suggest that, without the presence of human observers or other stressful distractions, female praying mantises are far less likely to eat their partner than was previously thought, and that in fact this cannibalistic behaviour may even be uncommon in the wild. One theory is that, in a more natural, relaxed environment, mantises are more likely to employ elaborate courtship rituals, which somehow switch off the female's murderous instincts.

Do female lizards prefer an attractive male, or a nice rock?

Lizards are cold-blooded, which means they can't generate their own internal heat, and so instead depend on the heat of the sun. This is why lizards are usually found in hot climates, where they can bask in the sun's heat. The side-blotched lizard is found in California, where it favours rocky outcrops, which are ideal for sunbathing. On these outcrops, the most highly prized spots are those that have boulders on them, for the lizards to bask on.

For a lizard, boulders are desirable for a number of reasons. They are elevated, which means they get the sun first, and remain illuminated for longer at dusk. They retain their heat for a long time, so they remain warm even after the sun does go down, or in. They usually have crevices underneath them where a lizard can hide from predators, or shelter from the sun if the heat becomes too oppressive, or where a female can safely leave her eggs.

Since these boulders are highly prized, the males will

compete vigorously for them. For not only will a well-appointed boulder provide all the benefits mentioned above, it is also a key factor in attracting a female. When the time comes to mate, the females will gravitate towards those males who have the best basking spot.

However, this raises an interesting question. Are the females primarily attracted to the strong, vigorous male, who just so happens to have ownership of a choice piece of real estate? Or, rather, are they mainly looking for the boulder of their dreams, regardless of which male happens to be its occupant? To answer this question, one simply has to remove some of the high-value boulders from the territory of a dominant male, and move them into the previously boulderless outcrop held by a low-ranking lizard. Experiments of this type have been conducted, and it turns out that within days of being given the prime boulders, the weakling becomes swamped with female attention, while the alpha male noticeably loses his appeal. As any jeweller will tell you, some girls just can't resist a good-sized rock.

Which spider bites off his own penis?

Well, 'penis' is not quite accurate, because spiders don't exactly have a penis – instead, they have something called a pedipalp. Actually, that's not quite right either, since spiders have two pedipalps, not one. And, come to mention it, 'spiders' isn't quite accurate, either, since what we call 'spiders' are actually ants that have learned to glue on a pair of extra legs and build webs. OK, that last one was a lie.

But spiders really do have two pedipalps, which are specially adapted legs that they fill with sperm, and then insert into the female. A pedipalp is not considered to be a penis, for a number of reasons. For one thing, it doesn't actually fill with sperm in a conventional sense – rather, the spider oozes its sperm onto a special web, and then sucks it up into the pedipalp. During copulation, the spider inserts the pedipalp into the female's corresponding slot, where it twists and locks in place, and pumps in the sperm. Often, the pedipalp snaps off once the copulation has taken place.

In one species of spider, the tent cobweb weaver, the male deliberately chews off one of his pedipalps. He does this because he is tiny, and each of his pedipalps makes up 10 per cent of his body weight. When competing with other males for opportunities to mate, it is important to be fast and nimble, so he sacrifices one of these organs to gain an increase in speed and mobility. Males with just one pedipalp can run 44 per cent faster, for 63 per cent longer, and 200 per cent further, than those with a full complement. Therefore, chewing off a pedipalp can significantly increase the spider's opportunities for mating.

Really, though, you have to wonder whether it's worth it. Not only do they have to chew off their own todger just to get a bit of female attention, but even if they do get lucky, they usually end up dying on the job!

Why does the female blanket octopus ignore the male?

There are four species of blanket octopus, which are found in the waters around Australia's northern coast. They are remarkable creatures in a number of respects. They are one of only a tiny number of sea creatures that have nothing to fear from the Portuguese man o' war, which has a very painful and very poisonous sting. Blanket octopuses are immune to this poison, and the female will even rip tentacles from the Portuguese man o' war, to brandish as a weapon.

Another fascinating thing about blanket octopuses is how they mate. The female can grow to over 2 metres (6.5 feet) long, but the male is the size of a walnut, just 2.4 centimetres (about an inch). This means that the female is a hundred times bigger than her mate, and weighs around forty thousand times as much. When the male finds a

female, he tears off one of his tentacles and fills it with sperm. He hands it to the female, who then uses it to fertilise her eggs. She then carries on about her business, while he is left to float away and die. So, to answer the question, the reason the female ignores the male is that she can barely see him!

The third remarkable feature of the blanket octopus is that, unlike most octopuses, it does not produce ink to defend itself. Instead, it waves a large membrane, like a big cape, which billows in the water, and greatly increases the octopus's apparent size. It's this unusual technique that gives the blanket octopus its name.

How do fairy wrens avoid the damaging consequences of incest?

The superb fairy wren fully deserves its name, as it is one of Australia's most attractive and colourful birds. The male has a bright sapphire head, with a jet-black bar around his eye, which extends into a glossy black patch on the back of his neck. As in many similar species, the female is a relatively plain brown. These birds live in the bush country, where there is limited food and few suitable sites for nests. Consequently, families tend to stay together, and work collaboratively to make the most of the available resources.

One downside of this is that most of the pairings that take place are between relatives: fathers mate with daughters, mothers mate with sons, brothers mate with sisters, and so on. Of course, birds don't have any moral objection to incest; in fact, it is very common. However, it can carry a genetic cost, since it means that the gene stock becomes weakened, and the species has less scope for variation and evolution.

The fairy wrens have developed a fascinating solution to this problem. They are socially monogamous, but sexually promiscuous. In other words, although they do form stable romantic pairs, both partners will also mate with other individuals, from outside their territory, and will some-times even contribute to raising the resulting young. When a male travels to a neighbouring territory, he will show off his plumage with a range of coquettish flourishes. He may even carry a flower in his beak, to add to the effect. He may present this flower to a female, but he gives flowers only to these other lovers, never to his own long-term partner.

Using his array of charms, the male may copulate with as many as ten different females in a season. Similarly, his partner may take up to six additional mates, as well as allowing her main partner to copulate with her just often enough to keep him interested and feeding the chicks. However, one consequence of the pair's licentious behaviour is that sometimes none of these chicks will actually be his.

Which female fish has eight testes?

The female anglerfish is one of the marvels of the deep. 'Anglerfish' is a generic term, which actually refers to around three hundred different species, including sea toads, frogfish, batfish and monkfish. What they all have in common is that the females each have a long flexible appendage, like a fishing rod, which grows out of the middle of their head, and dangles in front of their face. At the end of this rod is something called an esca, which can be wriggled so that it looks like live bait.

With this clever device, the anglerfish attracts its prey. When a curious fish gets too close, tempted by the wriggling bait, the anglerfish devours it with its enormous mouth, which has huge, inward-facing teeth, to prevent the prey from escaping. Deep-sea anglerfish are even more extraordinary. Their esca can actually light up, thanks to a chemical reaction caused by the bacteria that live on it. In the depths of the ocean, they attract their prey using this amazing cold light.

Sadly, however, the male anglerfish is a somewhat less impressive character. He has no rod, no esca, and no light. He is tiny compared with the female, and practically incapable of finding food for himself. Many male anglerfish never eat a meal in their lives, as they manage to literally feed off their partner. As you might therefore imagine, finding a female is a male anglerfish's main priority. He has giant eyes, with which to find her, and huge nostrils, to seek out her pheromones. When he finds her, he bites into her side, and gradually starts to merge his body into hers. Within a few weeks, all of his body will be completely subsumed into hers, apart from his testes, which will remain dangling from her side, and supplying her with sperm. Some females have been found with as many as eight testes hanging from their sides.

Do any animals sell sex?

Indeed they do. Animal prostitution has been observed in at least two species of bird. The female purple-throated hummingbird will copulate with males, even outside the breeding season, in return for being allowed to find food in their territory.

Adélie penguins will also sell sexual favours in return for a precious commodity – in this case, stones. These Antarctic penguins build nests that are simply piles of stones, which serve to keep their eggs elevated, and therefore safe from the flooding that occurs in spring when the snow melts. However, only nests of a decent size are likely to be sufficient to protect the eggs from the waters, but in the Antarctic stones are hard to come by.

Therefore, when her partner's back is turned, the female Adélie penguin will offer sexual favours to others males, in return for high-value stones. Sometimes, these males will be so satisfied by her attentions that she will be able to come

back for more stones without having to provide sex, merely a little light petting. One female was observed collecting sixty-two stones in this way.

Which creature's mating ritual involves the male and female urinating in each other's faces?

Mating poses a particular problem for aggressive predators. On the one hand, they need to get close enough to one another to copulate. However, if the usual pattern is for rivals to attack each other on sight, they need to find a way to signal that on this particular occasion they are in fact feeling amorous, rather than aggressive.

Lobsters do this by using their urine. They have two bladders, which are located in their head, which means they can squirt urine into the face of a potential mate. When the male wants to mate, he will lie in his shelter, urinating out of the entrance. The female may approach, and, if she's feeling receptive, she will urinate back at him. This urine seems to communicate that they are both ready to mate, and so they do. He flips her onto her back, and then climbs on top, prising her sperm pouch open using his rear legs. After mating, he will then guard her for around a fortnight, after which they will go back to normal, once again attacking one another on sight.

Scorpions face a similar problem when it comes to courtship, as they are usually very aggressive towards one another, but they resolve it in a far more elegant way. When the male finds a potential partner, he will rock back and forth in front of her, perhaps testing the ground. As she gets closer, he strikes at her with his tail, but with the sting safely tucked away. She fights back, and then they both bring their pincers forward, and start to dance together, for as long as half an hour, in what is known as the *promenade à deux*. At a given moment, he will bring his tail forward and inject her with a small amount of his venom, which seems to tranquillise her.

They continue to dance, and their faces get closer and closer, until they meet in a kiss, as the male kneads his mouthparts onto hers. By now, he will have found the kind of surface he has been looking for, which is at least part of the reason for the dance that has taken place. He sticks a tiny spike into the ground. It is a capsule that contains his sperm. He then pulls the female forward, until her genital opening is over the spike, at which point the spike releases sperm into her opening. Once this is done, they separate, perhaps because, now that the mating is over, there is a danger that she will try to eat him.

What is unusual about the romantic preference of the female quail?

Across the animal kingdom, the characteristics that females find attractive are enormously diverse, from elaborate horns and tusks, to iridescent feathers, to ornate and colourful nests. However, the vast majority of these traits tend to have certain things in common: they all suggest that the male will be healthier, stronger, and less prone to disease than his rivals.

However, the female quail is something of a rarity. Unlike most female creatures, she is more attracted to weaker males, rather than stronger ones. Scientists have found that male quails who routinely lose fights with rivals are more appealing to the females. This is a highly unusual strategy, which is not yet fully understood. One theory is that, because quails are by nature vicious and aggressive birds, the female chooses a weaker male to avoid the risk of being injured by a particularly aggressive partner.

Who is Lonesome George?

In the middle of the sixteenth century, human beings first discovered the Galápagos Islands, which are found in the Pacific Ocean near the equator, around 1000 kilometres west of Ecuador. They are now perhaps most famous as the scene of some of Charles Darwin's earliest observations of natural selection. When Darwin went to the Galápagos in 1835, there were around twelve different species of tortoise found on the archipelago, which meant four had already been rendered extinct. Today, there are just ten species remaining, one of which is comprised of a single individual, described in *The Guinness Book of World Records* as the world's rarest living creature: Lonesome George.

Lonesome George is a giant Pinta Island tortoise, who is believed to be between ninety and a hundred years old, and is almost certainly the last of his species. Since 1972, he has lived at the Charles Darwin Research Station on Santa Cruz Island. Before George was discovered, the species was thought to have already died out. Since then, scientists have been desperately trying to find a female Pinta Island tortoise for him to breed with, but so far the quest has been in vain. Another option is to breed George with a female of a similar species, in the hope that the union will result in a Pinta Island tortoise offspring, but for years he has refused to mate with any of the giant females presented to him.

Until recently, that is. For on 21 July 2008 it was revealed that one of George's lady friends had laid thirteen eggs. These female tortoises are of a similar, but different, species to George. Before this point, George had refused to mate for all of his thirty-five years in captivity. Sadly, a few months later, all of the eggs turned out to be infertile, but at least it raised hopes that George was now prepared to mate.

And so it proved, for a year later, George did it again! On 21 July 2009, a second clutch of eggs was laid, this time comprising five. These have now been moved to an incubator, and it won't be known until December 2009 whether or not they are fertile.

Which bird spoils his mistress, while neglecting his wife?

The great grey shrike breeds in northern parts of Europe, Asia and North America, and then winters further south in each continent. It is a medium-sized grey bird with a black stripe across its eye and a white chest. Great grey shrikes usually form stable mating pairs, which the males reinforce by giving gifts to their partner, presenting them with a tasty insect, rodent, lizard, or even another bird. The male presents gifts before copulation, which suggests that the ritual is an important part of the mating process.

However, these birds are not entirely faithful. Some males will have a fling with another bird, and, when they do, they will generally give their mistress much more valuable gifts than they give to their partner back at home. In a study, unfaithful males were found to give their mistress gifts which contained, on average, four times as much energy, as well as taking much longer to catch, than the gifts they gave to their loyal partner.

Which frog glues himself to the female?

Frogs are slippery characters. They have very soft, delicate skin, which has to be kept moist. To protect their skin, frogs have special glands that produce a kind of slimy mucus, which keeps the skin moist while the frog is out of water, and waterproofs it when the frog is in the water. This mucus also protects frogs from predators, as it makes them slippery, and difficult to get hold of.

However, the downside of being very slippery is that it does make the business of mating rather difficult. It must be quite frustrating to have finally wooed your partner, only for her to slip out of your grasp because you're too greasy.

To deal with this problem, most male frogs have special

pads on the inside of their thumbs and fingers, to help them keep a firm hold of their elusive partners. Some pads are warty, while others are somewhat spiky. A few males also have patches of rough skin on their chest, which also helps to hold the female in place.

However, one type of African frog, called the common rain frog, has developed an ingenious solution. He is considerably smaller than the female, which means gripping her in place isn't really an option. Instead, he emits a special type of glue from his skin, with which he sticks himself onto her back. This glue is insoluble in water and resistant to rain.

How do male butterflies hypnotise the females?

One might assume that the glorious, colourful patterns found on butterflies' wings are designed to attract a female, but in fact much of the time butterflies can barely see one another. They are very near-sighted, and bad at detecting anything at a distance. Their eyes can see almost a full 360 degrees, but not with any accuracy or sharpness. This is because their main priority is to avoid predators. Predators, on the other hand, tend to have a narrower range of view, but with much sharper vision, the better to hunt with. For example, birds of prey, such as eagles, have a narrow field of view, with forward-facing eyes, but incredible powers of precision and magnification.

A butterfly's colourful pattern is often not designed for other butterflies at all, but rather to scare off hungry birds, or else for camouflage. Instead, it is the male butterfly's iridescent wing scales that are used to attract the female. These are arranged in a specific pattern, and ridged to reflect ultraviolet light. When the male flutters his wings at close range, it creates a strobe effect of ultraviolet light, which, along with the heady scent of his pheromones, mesmerises the female.

Once a pair have mated, the male has a number of ways of preventing his partner from going off and mating with someone else. Some species, such as the queen butterfly, cover the female with a kind of dust, which contains chemicals that make it difficult for her to fly. This dust also interferes with her antennae, making it harder for her to sense other males in the vicinity. Other species, such as the green-veined white butterfly, transfer a chemical to the female which makes her unappealing to other males, and she herself then disseminates this chemical from special organs known as 'stink clubs'.

What is the most common cause of death among antechinuses?

The antechinus is a small, mouselike rodent that is native to Australia, Tasmania and New Guinea. Its mating season lasts for about two weeks in spring, and during this time the male becomes completely single-minded, devoting himself to nothing but endless sex. He will spend as much as twelve hours continuously copulating with a single female, and then go straight on to another one. During this mating period, he will not sleep or eat. Eventually, he finds himself completely worn out, and his health noticeably deteriorates from pure exhaustion. He becomes thin, bedraggled, and often diseased, with his hair falling out. By the end of the two weeks, he is completely spent, and he dies soon afterwards.

Which bird believes that three's company?

Eurasian oystercatchers enjoy an unusual kind of romantic life, as they frequently have three-way relationships. These always consist of one male and two females. However, there seem to be two distinct types of three-way relationship among these birds. In one kind, the three live happily and cooperatively together. The two females share a single nest, sit and preen their feathers together, and lay their eggs together. Their laying is even synchronised, so that they tend to lay each clutch a day or so apart. These females also frequently attempt to mate with one another, almost as often as they do with the male. In this kind of relationship, the male seems to have no particular favourite among the two females, and the three of them all defend the nest together.

However, Eurasian oystercatchers also produce a different kind of three-way relationship, one that is quarrelsome and hostile. In these relationships, each female has a separate nest, which she defends on her own, while the male defends a territory that includes both nests. The females lay eggs around two weeks apart, and attack one another throughout the day. In these relationships, the male has a clear favourite, and will devote most of his attention to her nest and her young, often neglecting the second nest and leaving it undefended.

The romantic arrangements of the dunnock are also somewhat unconventional. They depend to a large degree on the amount of food available in the dunnock's territory at that particular time. If there is a lot of available food, the female won't need much help from the male, and so he may mate with a number of partners, who all build nests in his territory.

However, if food is scarce, then the opposite may apply: the female will need the help of more than one male to gather enough food to feed her young. Consequently, she will take a second, junior male partner, which her first partner will tolerate. He remains the senior partner, and continues to defend the territory, and mate with her frequently and in the open. The secondary male takes a subservient role. He too gets to mate with the female, but only hidden away in the bushes, out of sight. When the senior male mates with the female, he has a special technique for ensuring that he will be the father of her offspring: he pecks at her cloaca, until she emits a small white droplet, which he inspects closely. This is the sperm from the junior male, and the senior male will not mate with her until it has been discharged.

How might a mite mate?

Mites have an extraordinarily unpleasant system of reproduction. Each mother produces a brood consisting of a single male and a number of females. These all hatch inside her womb, and then begin breeding with one another, while still inside their mother. Once the male has mated with all his sisters, they begin to eat their way out of their mother, feasting on her body tissues.

Eventually, they munch their way to the outside world, killing their mother in the process. The young male also dies soon afterwards, but the females survive and move away, having been inseminated by their brother, ready to continue the cycle.

How does the female sagebush cricket keep her mate from straying?

The sagebush cricket is found in North America. To attract a female, male sagebrush crickets sing vociferously. They do this in a surprising way. They have no lungs or vocal cords; instead, they produce their sounds using just their wings. Their forewings have a row of fine teeth along their edge like a saw, and they scrape these against the edge of the opposing wing. Their wings also have a small, taut, circular patch, like a drum skin, which vibrates with the sound and amplifies it.

The female cricket has ears on her forelegs, and these can precisely locate the direction from where the song is coming. When she finds a mate, she does something rather unusual. She climbs onto his back, and as the mating begins, she starts to eat his wings. He doesn't seem to object to this. On the contrary, he even lifts his wings up to give her better access, while he inseminates her. These wings are thick and nutritious, and make a good meal for the female, but, once they've been eaten, the male is never again able to sing his song of love.

Which kinky creature likes to tie up his partner during sex?

The European crab spider is one of the more common spiders found in English gardens. Like many species of spider, the male is smaller than the female, which means he has to be careful when it becomes time for mating, to avoid being eaten by her.

The solution favoured by the male crab spider is to tie up the female. First, he approaches her tentatively. When he gets close, he grabs one of her forelegs. At this point, she is likely to struggle, but he calms her by gently stroking her. Once she stops moving, the male begins to tie her up, by crawling all over her, covering her in a net of silk thread. He fastens this net to the leaf, petal, or whatever it is that she is sitting on. Once she is secured, he approaches her from behind, lifts up her abdomen, and crawls beneath her. Then, he inserts his pedipalps, one at a time, into her genital pores. Once copulation is completed, he is able to escape, without being devoured for afters.

Another species of spider does things somewhat differently, because in this species it is the female that likes to tie up the male. Males of this species, a European orb-web spider whose genus is called *Argiope*, are able to approach the female safely, and insert their pedipalp to begin copulation. However, while this takes place, the female gently wraps him in silk. Often, once mating is complete, he is able to break free of these bonds. However, if this is the second time he has mated that day, he may well be too exhausted to escape, and in these instances the female will eat him.

CHAPTER SEVEN

Vicious varmints

What's the best way to fight a crocodile?

Crocodiles are one of the most enduring species on Earth, and for good reason: they are ferocious predators. If you're faced with a crocodile, your best bet is to get away as quickly as possible. The fastest crocodiles can only run at 11 miles per hour, which is slower than most people can sprint, so on land a person should be able to run away from a crocodile. It could also help to run from side to side, since crocodiles are not good at making sharp turns. Furthermore, you should not be tempted to climb a tree to escape. Crocodiles are incredibly patient, and will wait under a tree for days if they are likely to get a good meal out of it.

However, these tips are only really useful if you're confronted with a crocodile on land, which is not the likeliest scenario. Crocodiles live and hunt in the water, and it's there that an attack is most likely to take place. If you're attacked by a crocodile in the water, it's said that the best thing to do is to attack its eyeballs with your fingers. Apparently, the crocodile will automatically open its jaws and let you go, since the eyes are the most sensitive part of its body.

A twenty-six-year-old man named Hillary Amuma recently tested this theory, when he was grabbed by a crocodile while fishing in the Tana River in Ethiopia. The crocodile grabbed his left thigh, and began to drag him into the water. Amuma says at that point he remembered the traditional Pokomo tribe method his grandfather taught him of how to fight a crocodile. He threw away his fishing gear, and jabbed his fingers into the crocodile's eyes. The animal let Amuma go, but then attacked again. Once more, Amuma attacked the crocodile's eyes, and this time he escaped. 'I just aimed my fingers at its eyes and the reptile became immobile,' he said. 'The Pokomo say a crocodile fears being touched in the eyes and, once that is done, it

becomes immobile and lets go. A real Pokomo man cannot be scared by a crocodile.'

What is the world's deadliest creature?

Strictly speaking, I suppose one could argue that all animals that can kill you are equally deadly, but some are certainly more menacing, more potent, more prolific, or simply more interesting than others. For example, the spitting cobra is perhaps the world's deadliest snake. It is found in India, where it kills more than fifty thousand people every year. It is extremely venomous, and very aggressive.

The cone shell is a small, attractive mollusc, which surprisingly turns out to be one of the most dangerous things in the sea. Touch it, and it will fire a venomous harpoon from the end of its shell, which can kill you in seconds.

Another of the ocean's most fearsome predators is the box jellyfish, which is also known as the sea wasp. It has tentacles 5 metres (16 feet) long, which it trails in the water. A sting from a box jellyfish can kill a person in just a few hours.

The poison-dart frogs of the Amazon rainforest may be tiny, but each one contains enough poison to kill around ten to twenty people. (*See also* 'Why are poison-dart frogs endangered?' in Chapter 4).

The world's deadliest spider is perhaps the funnel-web spider. Its venom can kill a person in less than fifteen minutes, and its fangs are strong enough to bite through leather gloves. It likes to live around human settlements, and will attack on sight.

However, for sheer number of deaths, no creature can come close to the humble mosquito. In the last two hundred years, mosquitoes have killed more people and animals than any other species, nation, or weapon on Earth, making them the deadliest creature known to man. Mosquitoes are bloodsuckers that carry microorganisms in their saliva which can cause malaria, dengue fever, encephalitis, yellow fever and other diseases. Each year, these diseases kill more than 3 million people worldwide. Mosquitoes are found all over the world, including in many cold climates. At certain times of the year, Eskimos have to cover their faces with mud to protect themselves from attack. And what's the most exciting mosquito fact of all? In our view, it's this one: mosquitoes can dodge raindrops.

Which spider wraps its prey to death?

Many spiders have elaborate and ingenious ways of catching their prey. Some build sticky webs for insects to walk into, or throw small webs over their prey. Others jump onto their prey, or chase it, or ambush it. One species builds a trapdoor, from which it suddenly appears as if from out of the earth. Another spider mimics ants, so that it can then eat them. One even hunts underwater. But once these predators have caught their prey, they all tend to kill it in the same, direct fashion: they bite it, paralysing it with their venom, and then eat the body, devouring it with their sharp, powerful fangs.

However, hackled orb-weaver spiders have no fangs, which means they have no way of paralysing their prey. Instead, to kill a single moth or beetle, this spider will weave more than 140 metres (460 feet) of silk, performing more than 28,000 individual movements, wrapping its prey tighter and tighter. This silk shroud becomes so tight that it breaks the insect's legs and forces its eyes into its head, often killing it outright. The hackled orb-weaver is the only spider known to crush its prey to death in this way.

Do giant squid ever sink ships?

For centuries, sailors have told scary stories about 'kraken', legendary sea monsters capable of dragging the biggest ships to the bottom of the ocean. Generally, these stories have been thought to be myths, but recent incidents have raised the possibility that stories about kraken may have referred to a real creature: the giant squid.

In 2003, a sailor named Olivier de Kersauson was attempting to break the world speed record for circumnavigating the globe, when his 34-metre (110-foot) trimaran came to a sudden stop in the middle of the Atlantic. When one of the crew looked through a porthole, he saw an enormous tentacle, thicker than a human leg, trying to get a grip on the yacht's rudder. The boat began to shake, but then the creature seemed to give up, and vanished back into the ocean. One of the crew reckoned the creature must have been about 10 metres long.

Although sea monsters of this size may sound improbable, evidence suggests that they may well exist. In the same year that de Kersauson's yacht was attacked, scientists in New Zealand found the remains of a squid that had been caught while attacking a trawler in the waters off Antarctica. It was believed to be a juvenile of the super-squid species, *Mesonychoteuthis hamiltoni*. According to the research team, the size of this individual suggested that a fully grown adult could reach as much as 15 metres (50 feet) in length. In 2004, researchers took the first pictures of a live adult giant squid in its natural habitat.

Which fish spits its prey to its death?

The archer fish has a very impressive technique for catching its prey. It is unique among fish, because it can shoot down its insect prey by squirting a precise jet of water from its mouth to knock them down from the waterside leaves and stems where they perch, to a height of up to 3 metres (10 feet). The archer fish is amazingly accurate, almost always hitting its target with the first shot. This is particularly impressive when you consider that the archer fish is underwater, which means that its view of the insect is refracted and distorted by the water's surface. Somehow, the fish takes this into account when it aims.

Then, within 100 milliseconds of the insect being knocked off its perch, the fish will start swimming to the exact spot in the water where it knows the insect will fall. Amazingly, the archer fish can predict this landing point so accurately that it arrives to collect the insect just 50 milliseconds after it hits the water, ensuring that no other predator can sneak in and steal the fish's meal.

Which bird kicks its prey to death?

The secretary bird has an unusual way of killing its prey: it stamps its victims to death. It is an extremely tall, gangly bird, which can reach 1.2 metres (4 feet) in height. It can fly if necessary, but it has largely lost the habit, probably because it is so successful at hunting on the ground. It stalks across the grasslands of Africa, often walking as far as 15 miles a day. Its main food is snakes, which it kills by kicking them in the head with its back toe, but it also eats a wide range of other ground-dwellers, including rats and insects.

Why do white-winged choughs kidnap the chicks of rival families?

The white-winged chough is native to Australia, and was named by early settlers after the European chough, which it resembles, although in fact the two species are not closely related. An individual white-winged chough is very much dependent upon its family. It does not reach sexual maturity until it is four years old, and until that time it will usually stay with its parents. This suits the parents well, because, as far as these birds are concerned, the bigger the family unit, the better.

The reason for this is that white-winged choughs survive by foraging in the leaf litter for insects, grubs, snails and grain. This is skilled, labour-intensive work. It takes young birds a long time to learn how to find food, as much as eight months, so it is useful for the family unit to have as many capable helpers around as possible. This is particularly important during the breeding season, when there may be as many as four new chicks to feed, none of whom will contribute significantly for a long while. For this reason, families of white-winged choughs generally need at least eight helpers if they are to raise all four of their hatchlings.

If a group manages to reach this kind of number, it may then try to expand its territory by declaring war on its neighbours. The family will go out as a group, including the immature young, and raid the territory of a neighbour, tipping its eggs and hatchlings out of the nest, and destroying the nest itself, which is an attractive, carefully crafted mud bowl.

The birds may also try to kidnap the newly fledged chicks of a rival group, by tempting them with offers of food. If a fledgling is persuaded by this, it will begin to accept the new family as its own within as little as half an hour. However, once a chough is a month old, it is no longer susceptible to being kidnapped, which suggests that the very young chicks do not yet fully recognise their own family.

Which wasp makes a spider spin it a cocoon?

There is a Costa Rican wasp, called *Hymenoepimecis argyraphaga*, which has an amazing way of getting its cocoon built. The process starts when the female wasp approaches a *Plesiometa argyra* spider. This is an enormous, fearsome spider, which most insects sensibly avoid, but not this one. Instead, the wasp hovers in front of the spider, and then lands directly on it. Then, it quickly brings its ovipositor forward, and implants an egg on the spider's back, before swiftly flying off.

The spider seems to be unharmed, but, as the egg develops, it remains on the spider's body, absorbing nutrients from its host. The night before the wasp larva pupates, the spider will destroy her own web. So far, this is fairly normal behaviour: most web-spinners regularly destroy their webs, eating the silk and thus recycling it.

However, at midnight, the spider will spin a new web, and this one will be very different from her usual orb web. This web has none of the usual features – no radial spokes, and no sticky spirals. Instead, it is attached to the surrounding plants by extra-strong, reinforced threads. Unknowingly, the spider is building the last web it will ever produce. Once it is completed, the spider sits motionless underneath it, and never moves again. The wasp larva has injected the spider with a chemical, which first altered its web-spinning behaviour, and now puts it to death.

The wasp larva now feasts on the spider's body, eventually dropping the dry, empty husk. At dawn, the wasp spins its own bright orange cocoon, which hangs inside the spider's final web, elevated and protected from ants and Costa Rica's heavy rainstorms.

What is the toughest creature in the world?

As we have seen, mosquitoes and poison-dart frogs are pretty deadly, but they couldn't be described as tough, and they are both fairly easy to kill. So which creature is the toughest, and most resilient? Is there a creature so tough that none of these venomous killers can threaten it? Which animal can survive the harshest conditions? Here are a few contenders for the title . . .

Grizzly bears are pretty tough. They have no natural predators, they can eat almost anything, and they can survive for up to six months without food during hibernation. Polar bears are also tough. They too have no predators, and manage to survive in one of the most inhospitable parts of the world, with temperatures as low as minus 37 degrees Celsius (minus 34.6 degrees Fahrenheit).

Armadillos may not be an obvious choice, but they are very hard to kill. Their armour is tough and leathery, making them impenetrable to predators as dangerous as wolves, coyotes and bears. However, jaguars can crack them open as they have immensely powerful jaws, which can generate over 300 kilograms (660 pounds) of pressure.

Of course, there are many kinds of toughness and resilience. Camels can lose as much as 25 per cent of the water in their bodies, and still survive the heat of the desert. Most animals, including humans, will die of thirst after losing just 10 per cent of their water. An African lungfish can survive for as long as four years without food. Scarab beetles can lift over four hundred times their own weight. They can even support eight hundred times their own weight on their back.

Cockroaches are famously resilient. A cockroach can survive being frozen, poisoned or even beheaded. A beheaded cockroach will eventually die, but only because it no longer has a mouth, and so it dies of thirst. Cockroaches can survive 6,400 rads of radiation – just 2,000 rads are enough to kill a human being. It can also survive a pressure of 126 Gs, while 18 Gs will kill a person. As a species, cockroaches seem practically indestructible. They have been around for 350 million years, and one female alone can produce half a million offspring a year.

However, in terms of toughness, one creature stands alone, and yet it's one that few people have heard of, and even fewer have actually seen. The tardigrade is a microscopic animal that grows to just over a millimetre in length, and looks a bit like a woodlouse. There are more than nine hundred species of tardigrade, and they are found almost everywhere on Earth; in lakes, oceans, and on land. They can swim or walk, and their loping bearlike gait is the reason for their other name: the water bear.

Despite their size, tardigrades are immensely tough. They can survive at temperatures lower than minus 250 degrees Celsius (minus 418 degrees Fahrenheit). They are effectively radiation-proof, and they can withstand pressures of more than 6,000 kilograms per square centimetre, which is more than six times greater than the pressure of sea water at a depth of 10,000 metres. They can survive being frozen, dehydrated, or even sent into space. When civilisation collapses, and all that's left is a post-apocalyptic wasteland, the tardigrade will endure.

What are siafu?

Siafu are one of the fiercest and most dangerous of all the insects. They are found mainly in Africa, where they live in large colonies, and are also known as driver ants, or

Matabele ants. They eat a varied diet which includes insects, earthworms, termites and sometimes much larger animals. Some ants have even been known to eat weak or injured mammals.

The siafu travel in raiding parties several hundred strong. They have enormous, shear-like jaws, which they carry pointing vertically downwards. They march in columns, about six abreast. Alongside the soldiers run minors, which are about half their size. Earlier, a scout will have laid down a scent trail to lead them to their target, which will often be a termite's nest. As they march, they 'sing', by rubbing a patch of ridges on their front.

When they reach the termite hill, they are faced by ranks of soldier termites. These are bigger than the siafu, with huge, armoured heads, and powerful jaws, but nonetheless they are no match for the siafu. The siafu seize the termites, and quickly inject their venom into the termite's brain, killing it within seconds. The raiders now start to make a pile of the vanquished termites.

With no guards left, the termite nest is now defenceless. The siafu storm inside, killing all the soft-bodied worker termites they can find. For a quarter of an hour, the slaughter may continue, as the pile of bodies grows. The minors now start to take the bodies back to their nest, carrying as many as six at a time. Eventually, the army march home, this time singing a different song, presumably a triumphant song of victory.

Do animals bear grudges?

Some intelligent animals do seem to be able to remember individuals who have somehow displeased them in the past, and behave differently towards them as a result. A recent study at the University of Florida found that mockingbirds could remember people who had previously threatened their nests, and would menace or even attack them. In the study, a group of volunteers approached the mockingbirds' nests, and gently touched the edges. They did this on a number of consecutive days, giving the mockingbirds time to remember their faces. After just two days, the birds started responding differently to those individuals they recognised, giving alarm calls earlier than usual, and even defending their nests with aggressive swooping dives, sometimes grazing the top of the volunteers' heads. Meanwhile, new volunteers would approach the nests, but the birds would remain calm. They only seemed to attack people they recognised from previous days.

There are also accounts of elephants bearing grudges. In Uganda in the 1980s, a large proportion of the elephant population were killed for their ivory. Some experts believe that those elephants who survived, many of whom would have been infants at the time, may have retained traumatic memories from their infancy, causing them long-term mental anguish into their adulthood. This has led to juvenile elephants terrorising motorists, and attacking towns and villages in what some believe to be revenge attacks.

In another, equally anecdotal example, an elephant in

a travelling circus was believed to have killed a woman over a lingering resentment. In Texas in 1928, the circus had come to town, and the trainer of an elephant named Black Diamond had begun a relationship with a local woman, who had encouraged him to leave the circus. The next year, when the circus returned, Black Diamond attacked the woman and killed her, in what many believed to be a deliberate act of revenge. They do say elephants never forget.

Which creature is the sloth's only predator?

Sloths are slow, sleepy creatures, who spend their days hanging and eating in the treetops, and could never be described as aggressive or threatening. Nonetheless, their unusual lifestyle means that they are practically invulnerable to predators. Except for one. For amazingly, even though a sloth can weigh as much as sheepdog, there is a type of bird that is capable of swooping down and carrying one off.

This bird is the amazing harpy eagle of South America, which can also prey on monkeys. As you might imagine, it is an enormous bird, with a wingspan of up to 7 feet (about 2 metres). It is an expert hunter, which swoops down through the trees to quickly snatch its prey. Its talons are as big as a grizzly bear's claws, and are capable of smashing the bones of its prey. They are also long, sharp, and deeply curved, and thus very difficult to escape from. When the harpy eagle swoops down to grab a monkey or a sloth, it does so by swinging its legs forcefully, stabbing its sharp talons right through the animal's body. The force of this blow is sometimes enough to kill the animal outright. If not, the resulting damage to its internal organs will usually finish off the job. When it lands with its prey, the harpy eagle tears it apart with its hooked beak, which is as sharp as a razor. It is an extraordinarily effective predator.

Which birds attack in squadrons?

Fieldfares are one of the largest members of the thrush family, and are found in Europe and northern Asia. They are fairly large birds, around 22–27 centimetres (about 9–10.5 inches) long, which feed on insects, berries and earthworms. They are sociable and collaborative birds, which often nest together in colonies. Like many birds, they alert one another to the arrival of a predator.

The first fieldfare to spot such a threat, for example a chick-stealer such as a magpie, will give a call, sounding the alarm. However, rather than simply rushing for cover, the rest of the birds will take up the cry themselves, so that it quickly becomes an unnerving cacophony. Then, they dive-bomb the predator, shrieking at it as they swoop down, before releasing a bomb of faeces. Fieldfares are very adept at aiming these bombs, and many of them will hit their target. The magpie may soon end up covered in faeces, making it fall to the ground, where it will hop away, dejectedly, to clean itself up.

Which crustacean has a hidden flick knife?

The mantis shrimp lives in shallow tropical and subtropical seas. It has an extension to its main claw that it keeps folded out of sight, a bit like a closed flick knife. When hunting, the mantis shrimp flicks open this claw extension at enormous speed, and smashes it into its prey. It is one of the fastest physical movements that any animal is known to produce. A large Californian mantis shrimp, which is about 25 centimetres (10 inches) long, can have a strike speed of 10 metres (33 feet) per second, which is about the speed of a bullet fired from a .22-calibre rifle. This strike is powerful enough to cut small fish in two, or crack open the shells of crabs and shellfish. Mantis shrimps are therefore not recommended as pets, because their amazing weapon has been known to crack the side of a double-walled safety-glass fish tank.

However, even the mantis shrimp is arguably outdone by the resourceful hermit crab, which actually uses other creatures as weapons. A hermit crab will attach a sea anemone to the back of its shell. Sea anemones are used for their vicious, stinging tentacles, which serve to keep any predators far away from the hermit crab.

The little boxer crab takes this innovation even further. It carries a small anemone in each of its two front pincers, and brandishes them like maces. If any predator threatens the crab, it thrusts its pincers forward, wielding its two bunches of stinging tentacles. The crab never lets go of its anemones, which means it is unable to use its front pincers to pass food into its mouth as most crabs do, so instead it has learned to use its two front legs for this purpose.

Why do male spiders give presents to the females?

In many species of spider, the female is much bigger than the male, and will eat him given half a chance. Male spiders therefore tend to stay out of the female's way, but when it becomes time to mate, they have no choice but to risk an approach. However, neither the prospect nor the act of copulation does anything to soften the female's belligerent attitude, which means that the male spider has to be alert to danger at every stage of the process. In one well-known example, the female black widow spider will sometimes kill and eat the male straight after mating.

To protect themselves from this fate, some species of spider have developed a range of crafty strategies. In some species, the male will bring the female a present to distract her. This present usually consists of a fly, or some other morsel of food, wrapped in a silk thread. While the female is busy unwrapping this parcel, the male will quickly mate with her. However, some males employ an even craftier trick. These devious Lotharios offer the female an empty husk, a wrapped gift with nothing inside it. By the time the female has opened the parcel and discovered that she's been deceived, the male will have already mated with her and escaped.

The male nursery web spider has developed an even more bizarre strategy for winning over the female. To attract a mate, he pretends to be dead. He stretches out his body, lying completely still, while holding a morsel of food in his mouth. The female comes to investigate the food, and may even grab it, dragging him with it. At this point the male will suddenly spring into action, and manoeuvre himself into the mating position. A recent study of nursery web spiders found that 89 per cent of males who played dead achieved copulation, while only 40 per cent of their more vivacious rivals were successful.

The redback spider does something even more extra-ordinary. Rather than trying to avoid being eaten, the male redback actually encourages the female to eat him. As in most spider species, the female redback is much bigger than the male. When mating begins, the male performs a kind of somersault over the female, so that his abdomen is directly over her mouthparts, encouraging her to devour him, while the copulation continues to take place. Odd as it may sound, this behaviour seems actually to help the male redback to reproduce, since males who get eaten by the female actually tend to mate for longer, and thus fertilise more eggs. Also, females who have already eaten one partner become less likely to go on to mate with another male. And you thought human dating was weird.

Which mammal, apart from humans, engages in kidnapping, gang rape and pointless murder?

The surprising answer is the dolphin, despite its sweet, caring reputation. Dolphins are one of the best-loved of all animals, and they are undeniably cute, playful and intelligent. Like us, dolphins live in social groups, of up to a dozen individuals, and establish strong social bonds. Dolphins look after sick or injured companions, and help them to the surface if they are having trouble breathing. Furthermore, dolphins don't reserve this altruistic behaviour solely for other dolphins: they have also been observed assisting a stranded pygmy sperm whale and her calf. They have also been known to protect humans from shark attacks, either by circling the human, or charging at the sharks.

However, dolphins also have a considerable dark side. Males often form groups of two or three individuals, seemingly for the sole purpose of forcing females into sex. A group of males will herd a female, sometimes for months at a time, with each of the members aggressively coercing her into sex. These groups also kidnap females from other, rival groups. This kind of aggressive sexual behaviour is not just directed towards other dolphins: there are also numerous reports of dolphins sexually molesting human beings. In 2002, swimmers in Weymouth, Dorset, were warned to avoid a bottlenose dolphin named George, who had learned to isolate female swimmers, circling them and leading them away from the group, before attempting to mate with them. Even celebrities aren't safe. While shooting the TV series *Flipper*, Jessica Alba was moved to request that in future she be paired only with female dolphins, after a number of males had tried to mate with her.

Dolphins are also surprisingly violent. Male bottlenose dolphins have been known to kill their own young. Aggression between rival males is common, and older males will usually have a number of battle scars. Some dolphin violence seems to have no obvious purpose. Dolphins have been seen attacking and killing porpoises, even though the two species have very different diets, and so are not competitors for food. Dolphins also gang up on smaller members of their own species. They begin by 'jaw clapping', producing an eerie, audible warning. They then attack in numbers, overwhelming the victim with bites, headbutts, and powerful blows from their tail fins.

In a wide-ranging study of dolphins which seek out human company, three-quarters were seen to display aggressive behaviour, sometimes leading to serious injury, and half took part in 'misdirected sexual behaviour', with boats and buoys, as well as humans.

CHAPTER EIGHT

Weird wonders

Why does the pinacate beetle stand on its head?

The pinacate beetle is a mean-looking black beetle that can reach up to 4 centimetres (1.5 inches) in length. It is extremely hardy and is found in great numbers in the deserts of the south-western USA and Mexico, where few other creatures can survive. Pinacate beetles are so common here that there is even a mountain range named after them, the Pinacate Mountains, on the border between Sonora and Arizona.

Pinacate beetles are also known as clown beetles, as they do something rather bizarre when faced with danger. Rather than run away, these beetles will hurriedly stand on their head, often tumbling over into a somersault if they fail to balance properly. A beetle may flip over a number of times before settling into a controlled headstand. However, although this display is entertaining, it's wise to take this as a warning, because, if the beetle continues to feel threatened, it may attack. It does so by shooting a disgusting, noxious chemical from its rear end, which it can fire up to 75 centimetres (30 inches). For this reason, pinacate beetles have another nickname: they are also commonly known as stink beetles. Stink beetle spray can cause painful burning and temporary blindness if its gets into your eyes, and it's extremely difficult to wash off.

However, a number of predators have figured out a way to take advantage of the stink beetle's abundance. Grasshopper mice teach their young a particular technique. They grab the beetle, and stick its rear end into the ground, where it can't do any harm. They then chew through the top half of the beetle. The beetle's other predators include burrowing owls, loggerhead shrikes, and, appropriately enough, skunks.

Which worm captures its prey by covering it with glue?

The answer is the velvet worm, which is a fascinating evolutionary relic. Despite the name, the creature is not velvety, and in fact it's not even a worm. It looks a bit like a caterpillar, with a long, segmented body and between 13 and 43 pairs of stumpy feet. Velvet worms are usually around 5 centimetres (2 inches) long, and are found in most tropical climates. However, they are very wary creatures, who avoid light, so they are rarely seen. They have a fascinating evolutionary history, since they are believed to have existed largely un-changed for 500 million years, and may represent an evolu-tionary link between arthropods – that's the group that includes insects and spiders – and annelids, such as earth-worms.

Velvet worms have porous skin, which means there is a constant risk of drying out. Consequently, they tend to live in dark, damp, secluded places such as caves, rotting logs, and leaf litter. Velvet worms are cute, colourful creatures, but they are also voracious predators. They hunt at night, often killing prey much larger than themselves, including crickets, termites, woodlice and spiders. They capture their prey by covering it in a sticky glue, which they shoot from two powerful tubes located next to their mouth. Velvet worms can fire this glue up to 30 centimetres (about a foot). As it flies, it dries in the air, before entangling the unfortu-nate victim, leaving it unable to escape. Then the worm will bite into its prey, injecting it with digestive saliva, to soften and liquefy its meal, before devouring the creature's insides. The velvet worm will also eat the glue, which is rich in protein. The worm's skin is waterproof, which is why it doesn't get stuck to the glue itself.

Velvet worms also reproduce in a rather unusual way. In a number of species, the male will place his sperm packet on his head, and present it to the female, like a trophy. Some velvet worm species have even developed elaborate structures on their heads to hold the sperm, including spikes, hollow stylets, and pits. The male then places his head against the female's rear end, and transfers the sperm packet into her genital opening.

Which bird drinks blood?

The vampire finch is one of the twelve finch species observed by Charles Darwin on the Galápagos Islands, which helped him to develop his theory of evolution by natural selection. Darwin noted that the various species of finch found on the islands seemed to be closely related, but that the shape and size of each species' beak seemed to be different from the others, and yet perfectly adapted for opening or reaching the main foodstuff found on each particular island.

Summing up his conclusions from the trip, he wrote, 'Seeing this gradation and diversity of structure in one small, intimately related group of birds, one might really fancy that from an original paucity of birds in this archipelago, one species had been taken and modified for different ends.'

One feature of the Galápagos Islands is that they are very dry, with a lack of fresh water. When there is occasional rain, the seeds produced by the islands' plants and trees get eaten soon afterwards. However, birds need water in their diet, so the vampire finch has found a number of ways to stave off thirst. First, it drinks nectar from the flowers of the Galápagos prickly pear. Second, it steals eggs, rolling them from their nests and onto rocks and smashing them, to drink the nourishing yolk inside.

The vampire finch's third method is even more extraordinary: it drinks the blood of other birds, usually masked boobies and red-footed boobies. It does this by pecking the skin in front of their tail until it bleeds. Surprisingly, the boobies don't seem to mind being pecked, as they offer little resistance. Some believe that this behaviour may have evolved from an earlier, mutually beneficial habit of picking parasites from the boobies' skin. Over time, the finches may have inadvertently begun to draw blood, and continued the practice, as the nutritious blood became a key source of protein and liquid.

There is another type of bird, the oxpecker, which does something similar. Oxpeckers are found in Africa, and feed exclusively on the backs and necks of large mammals including cattle, rhinos, buffalo, antelopes, impalas and giraffes. It used to be thought that oxpeckers enjoyed a mutually beneficial relationship with their hosts – the theory was that the oxpeckers cleaned the large mammals' skin, by pecking away ticks, botfly larvae, and other parasites, often from hard-to-reach spots such as inside the animal's nostrils or ears.

However, recent research suggests that, like vampire finches, oxpeckers may simply be parasites, who may once

have helped to clean their hosts, but now subsist chiefly by reopening wounds, and feeding on the animal's blood. It is true that oxpeckers do remove some ticks and larvae from their hosts, but evidence suggests that they may not remove enough of them to actually make any meaningful difference.

How does a snake swallow an antelope?

Snakes are some of the most astonishing predators on Earth. There are more than 2,900 species of snake, and all of them are carnivorous hunters, despite their apparent lack of advantages. Snakes have no legs for chasing their prey, no hands for grabbing it, and no teeth for chewing. Most species of snake can't even see particularly well. And yet they are found on every continent except Antarctica, and they prey on animals many times their size, including cats, pigs, and even antelope. How do they do it?

Most snakes kill their prey in one of three ways. Some use constriction, wrapping their body around the prey, tightening the grip every time the victim exhales, until eventually it is unable to breathe in. Some kill using their venom. More often, however, snakes use their venom only to paralyse and subdue their prey, before swallowing it whole.

Snakes are able to swallow creatures more than three times larger than their own head, which is roughly equivalent to us being able to swallow a basketball whole. A snake is able to do this because its skin and body are extremely elastic, and its skeleton has no pectoral girdle to limit the size of food that can be passed down its body. Snakes can also open their jaw to as much as 130 degrees, whereas the human jaw can only reach a maximum angle of 30 degrees. However, the common belief that snakes can dislocate their jaw is actually a misconception. In fact, a snake's jaw does not detach, but it is rigged with tendons, muscles and ligaments, which give it enormous flexibility. A snake's lower jaw comprises two halves, left and right, which are connected by a flexible, elastic ligament, allowing them to be stretched apart.

Snakes have no teeth to chew with, so they have to swallow their food whole. They swallow their prey head first, because creatures such as birds, hedgehogs and goats have feathers, spines, and horns, which could provide resistance or injury if ingested the wrong way round. Snakes have strong cheek and throat muscles, with which they push their prey down to the stomach, in a process that can take several hours.

Once the food reaches the stomach, the process of digestion can begin. If the meal is a big one, digestion can take a long time. Sudden movements may be risky if the meal includes spiky things such as spines, claws, or horns, so the snake will now try to lie low, out of the way, moving as little as possible.

A large meal causes the snake's body to undergo substantial changes to facilitate the process of digestion and storage. Its heart will swell by 40 per cent, and its liver may double in size. It can take more than a week for a snake to digest a large meal. Then, when digestion is finally completed, the snake's internal systems enter a dormant state, with significantly reduced functions, to conserve energy.

In this way, snakes can swallow creatures many times their size. An African rock python was observed swallowing a 59 kilo (130 pound) antelope. There are also reports of snakes swallowing alligators whole, and even human beings. In one recent example, in Indonesia an entire human body was said to have been cut out of a reticulated python, covered in slime and digestive juices.

How does an octopus walk?

Octopuses are cephalopods, a class of molluscs that also includes squid and cuttlefish. Octopuses have eight arms (or tentacles), and no internal or external skeleton. They are regarded as the most intelligent of the invertebrates, and have a number of ways of defending themselves against predators, including fleeing, hiding, camouflaging themselves by changing colour and shape, and expelling ink, creating a thick, black cloud around themselves.

Octopuses usually move around by either crawling on their many arms, or swimming, using jet propulsion, expelling a jet of water which they aim using a muscular siphon. However, two recently discovered species use a different and ingenious method of getting around: they walk bipedally, on just two of their arms. They are called the coconut octopus and the algae octopus, and as their names suggest, the reason for their bizarre mode of getting around is that it is part of their camouflage. They wrap their other six arms around their body, disguising themselves as, respectively, a fallen coconut, tumbling along the ocean floor, and a lump of algae or seaweed.

Which fish is more closely related to human beings than it is to herring?

On 23 December 1938, Hendrik Goosen, the captain of the fishing trawler *Nerine*, returned to harbour at East London, South Africa. He phoned his friend, Marjorie Courtenay-Latimer, who was a curator at a local museum, to tell her he had found an unusual fish that she might be interested in looking at.

When she got there, the fish was not one she recognised, and she could find no record of it in her books. She showed it to a friend, Professor James Leonard Brierley Smith, and he immediately recognised it as a coelacanth (pronounced SEE-luh-kanth), a fish that was believed to have been extinct for 80 million years. Since 1938, there have been many more sightings of coelacanths, up the east coast of Africa as far as Kenya, and in the waters around Indonesia.

Amazingly, there are fossil records of coelacanths going back as far as 400 million years ago, which means that they predate even the dinosaurs. The coelacanths found today

are regarded as 'living fossils', because they remain un-
changed from fossil specimens that date back to 80 million
years ago. Coelacanths are part of a group of lobe-finned
fish that are believed to be the ancient ancestors of all
four-limbed vertebrates, which, astonishingly, means that
coelacanths may be more closely related to you and me
than they are to herring.

How do you make a dino-chicken?

Evidence suggests that the most likely living descendants
of dinosaurs are birds; in fact, it would be accurate to say
that birds are highly evolved theropod dinosaurs. However, this does not mean that birds are evolved from flying
dinosaurs such as pterodactyls – strictly speaking, pterodactyls were not dinosaurs at all. Instead, birds evolved
from bipedal, ground-dwelling dinosaurs, which over time
developed feathers.

Initially, these feathers were probably useful only for
keeping warm, but over time they evolved to help the dinosaurs jump higher to catch insects, to glide rather than
fall, and then eventually to fly. Over time, these dinosaurs
gradually lost their teeth, which were replaced by smooth,
aerodynamic beaks.

How can scientists know this, when dinosaurs died out
65 million years ago? Well, the first clue is that theropod
dinosaurs shared many features with today's birds. Like
birds, they had feet with three toes, bones filled with air,
a wishbone, and in some cases feathers and eggs. Also,

scientists have found numerous fossils of strange 'dino-birds', intermediate dinosaur-like creatures, which have feathers and the beginnings of wings. Furthermore, geneticists have even been able to reactivate dormant dinosaur genes in some birds, including chickens, causing them to grow sharp teeth inside their beaks, creating weird and scary-looking dino-chickens.

Why do vultures have bald heads?

There are two distinct families of vulture, and, despite their many apparent similarities, the two are not closely related to each other. They demonstrate nature's amazing ability to evolve similar solutions to similar problems, quite separately, so that creatures with similar lifestyles often look very similar, even when the two species are unrelated. The two families of vulture evolved entirely separately, on different continents. African vultures are related to hawks and eagles, while South American vultures are related to storks. There are major internal differences in their skeletons and musculature that clearly demonstrate this.

However, although they may not be related, they live and hunt in very similar ways and, consequently, they have evolved many physical similarities. Both types of vulture have broad, blunt-ended wings, which allow them to glide on the hot thermals that rise from the grassy savannahs where they hunt. And both have bald heads, because they feed by pushing their heads deep inside the bloody corpses of dead animals. If they had feathers on their heads, these would soon become matted with blood and guts, and attract parasites and infection. Surprisingly perhaps, vultures are actually very clean birds, and will always take a bath after a meal if they can, and will travel long distances to find water.

Their bald heads may also serve another useful purpose. Both families of vulture live in very hot climates, but spend much of their time at high altitudes, where the temperature is very low. As a result, they need to have thick feathers on their body to keep warm, but on the ground these feathers make the birds uncomfortably hot. Their bald heads, exposed to the air, may go some way to helping them cool down.

Why are penguins black and white?

Penguins are naturally comic creatures, which have an enduring appeal for humans, thanks no doubt in part to their amusing and distinctive appearance, which manages to be simultaneously cute and absurd. But what is the reason for their unmistakable black-and-white feathers, which make them look like a pompous wine waiter?

Well, it may look a little daft on land, but actually a penguin's coat is extremely practical. It protects them from predators. The penguin's predators are sharks, killer whales, and seals, each of which can only pose a threat in the water. A penguin's coat helps to camouflage it while swimming. From above, its black back is hard to make out against the darkness of the ocean. From below, its white front is hard to pick out against the white of the sky.

The penguin's distinctive colouring is also useful for managing the bird's temperature, which is of vital importance for a creature living in the frozen Antarctic. When a penguin is cold, it will turn its black back to the sun, to soak up as much of its warmth as possible. Then, when it gets too hot, as unlikely as this may sound, the penguin can turn its white belly to the sun, to reflect the heat.

Why don't woodpeckers get a headache?

Woodpeckers hunt for insects that few other birds can reach, hidden beneath the bark of trees. They do this by pecking at the bark with great force: each blow hits the tree at around 25 miles per hour, and they peck up to 20 times per second. These blows are so powerful that, if the bird's beak were not locked together by a special clasp, the two mandibles would fly apart.

A single one of these powerful whacks could knock the woodpecker unconscious, if its force were to reach the bird's brain, but luckily the woodpecker's head is cleverly designed to cushion the blow. Woodpeckers have muscles at the base of their beak that act as shock absorbers.

Furthermore, woodpeckers' brains are very small, and suspended in fluid. Consequently, none of the impact reaches the brain, and so the woodpecker remains conscious.

Woodpeckers also have clever ways to protect themselves from flying splinters. Their nostrils are tiny slits, which are protected by special feathers. And, to stop splinters getting in their eyes, woodpeckers close special membranes over their eyes a millisecond before each peck hits the wood.

Which bird can see even with its eyes closed?

The potoo is an enormous bird that can reach more than half a metre (1.6 feet) in height. It is found in the American tropics, and is related to the nightjar. Despite its size, even in broad daylight a potoo is almost impossible to see, because it has an amazing camouflage. The bird usually perches on top of a tree stump. It has brown, mottled feathers, which blend in perfectly with the tree's bark. If a predator approaches, the potoo takes further steps to make itself invisible. It lowers its tail, pressing it flat against the bark of the stump, so that there is no visible join. It then lifts its head upwards, so that its beak is pointing vertically, making it look just like a broken end of branch, and closes its eyes.

Closing its eyes suggests that the potoo has amazing confidence in its camouflage, especially as it will stay completely still, even letting a predator get within a metre of it, without moving. However, the potoo is not quite displaying blind faith in the way it may seem. Although its eyelids are shut, the bird can still see faintly, because its eyelids have two tiny vertical slits in them, which let through just enough light for the potoo to keep an eye on any approaching threat. If a predator does get too close for the potoo's comfort, it will suddenly take off and fly away. It must make quite a startling sight, to see a broken tree stump suddenly take flight!

What is unusual about the naked mole rat?

Well, for a start, it is not a mole, or a rat, or even naked, as it has whiskers and hairy toes. Apart from its blundering nomenclature, which to be fair is hardly the animal's fault, the naked mole rat is also unusual in the way that it looks, since it is perhaps the ugliest creature in the world. It looks like a pink flaccid penis, with squinty eyes and protruding buck teeth. Luckily, it spends its life in darkness!

Apart from the way they look, naked mole rats are also fascinating for many other reasons. They are found in eastern Africa, particularly Ethiopia, Kenya and Somalia. They are the only mammals that live in organised colonies, like ants or bees. A mole rat colony may comprise as many as three hundred adults, all pushing and shoving one another in the dark.

Like ants and bees, mole rat colonies have a queen, and she is the only female who gets to reproduce. She does so every eleven weeks, producing a litter of between ten and twenty-seven pups. Once the pups are born, the colony's workers take over all the feeding and raising duties. When the young mole rats reach three months old, they are put to work. Naked mole rats like to eat tubers, such as potatoes, and roots. They spend a lot of time trying to find these, and when they do they treat them with great care. They will gnaw a small hole in the tuber's rind, and then carefully hollow it out from the centre, leaving most of the outer skin intact. Then, they pack dirt up against the tuber, and leave the plant to recover.

The queen spends much of her time bullying and harassing the other females in the colony. This constant stress impedes their ability to reproduce, along with a special hormone in the queen's urine that makes the female workers sterile. If removed from the colony, a sterile worker will become sexually active within a week. A queen can live for twenty-five years, producing more than a thousand offspring. When she dies, there is vicious fighting between the biggest females as they compete to become the next queen.

Which butterfly has a false head?

The hairstreak butterfly has a false head on its hindwings, to confuse predators. The false head distracts birds from the butterfly's actual head, and confuses them when the butterfly escapes, seemingly flying backwards.

In fact, there are a number of other creatures that have false heads, which seem to be similarly effective in confusing and deterring predators. The shingleback lizard, for example, has a large, stumpy tail, which is exactly the same size and shape as its head.

There is also an amazing type of frog found in Chile, Brazil and Uruguay that uses its entire body as a false head. The appropriately named four-eyed frog has two large swellings on its sides, which look just like eyes. They sit just above the frogs' legs, and the overall effect is that the frog's whole body looks like the head of a much larger, more threatening creature. Additionally, these false eyes are actually poison glands, so even if a predator does decide to bite the frog, the unpleasant taste will usually make it let go pretty quickly.

Which bird has a uniform?

You don't have to be a dedicated twitcher to know that birds have coloured markings that are literally specific – they identify the bird by its species. This is important for birds that may, in all other respects, look just like birds of different species. Many small songbirds, for example, are indistinguishable from one another, except for their colourful markings. And, since it's crucial for birds to find a mate of the same species, these markings serve an important function.

However, a bird's markings are also useful in other ways. In some birds, the size and shape of markings can indicate status or seniority, like the stripes on a soldier's uniform. For example, all male house sparrows have a black bib, but some bibs are larger than others. Collared flycatchers have a white patch on their forehead, and this varies in size. Male great tits have a black stripe that runs down their chest, and some of these stripes are thicker than others. In each case, the bigger the patch or stripe, the more senior the bird.

The size of a bird's markings are a product of both its genes and its lifestyle. Strong, aggressive parents are likely to pass their strength and aggression on to their offspring, along with their distinctive physical characteristics. Additionally, birds that are strong and healthy are likely simply to have bigger chests than weaker birds, and so their coloured bibs will naturally appear bigger. Young collared flycatchers hatch in Europe, and at this point in their lives they have no white patch on their forehead. They develop this patch only when they moult, while wintering in Africa. The size of the patch is determined by how well they feed there, making it an accurate indication of their physical strength.

These markings are useful because many small birds are aggressive and territorial, but clear indications of strength and seniority minimise the need for the birds to actually fight and risk injury. If they carry markings that clearly indicate which bird is likely to win the fight, the weaker bird can submit, saving itself from unnecessary pain or injury.

Which frog has a visible, beating heart?

There is a tiny frog called the glass frog, which is found in many parts of Central and South America. Glass frogs range from around 3 to 7 centimetres (about 1–2.5 inches) in length, and look a bit like tree frogs, with attractive lime-green skin on their backs. However, if you turn the frog over, you will see something quite astonishing. The skin on the glass frog's front is transparent, allowing you to see its internal organs at work: its liver, digestive tract, and even its beating heart and circulating blood.

What happens at a dung beetle wedding?

Dung beetles love one thing above all others: poo. When a dung beetle finds a tempting pile of droppings, it sifts through it, looking for the choicest morsels. Having made its selection, the beetle will then start to roll its dung into a ball, which soon becomes considerably bigger than the beetle itself. It can roll a ball that is fifty times its own weight. How, you may wonder, does it roll something so much bigger than itself? The answer is that it climbs on top of the ball, and manipulates it with its legs.

Once the dung ball is complete, the next job is to roll it home. Again, this is done by balancing on top of the ball, and skilful beetles can roll their dung ball at speeds of up to 14 metres (46 feet) a minute. They need to travel quickly, because dung is a precious commodity. Other dung beetles may well come along and try to steal it. The dung beetle may have to fight for its dung. To minimise the risk of being robbed, dung beetles will always travel in a straight line towards their burial hole. Amazingly, they navigate by using polarised light from the moon. With luck, the beetle will manage to bring its prize home, to a safe burial spot, ready to provide a delicious source of food for many days.

However, there is more to dung than just a delicious

foodstuff. Every aspect of dung beetle society revolves around poo. When a pair of dung beetles get together, the male will often woo the female by presenting her with a ball of dung. Together, they then roll the ball back to their new home, with him pushing and her pulling, in a bizarre kind of wedding ceremony. Then, once the female has been fertilised, she lays her eggs inside the dung ball. The beetle larvae grow inside the ball, which provides an abundant source of food for their growth, before they eventually eat their way out.

What is unusual about the female fossa?

Fossas are medium-sized mammals, which are closely related to the mongoose. They are found only on Madagascar, where they are the dominant carnivore on land. The female fossa does something quite surprising: she appears to grow a penis. Just like the male fossa's penis, the female's has bone inside it, and is covered with nasty, backward-facing spikes. It leaks a bright orange discharge, just like the male's penis. The female even grows two large bumps on her genitals, which look just like testicles. However, once the female reaches maturity, at four years old, her 'penis' shrinks back to normal size. What appeared to be a penis was in fact the female's clitoris.

So why do the females grow a phony phallus? What possible benefit could it bring? One theory is that it helps to deter unwanted attention from males. Fossa copulation is an extremely rough and violent business, which can last for up to three hours, and involves licking, biting and screeching, all the time perched at the top of a tree, while the male's spiky penis locks him in place. Since the females are not ready to reproduce until they are four years old, it may well make sense for them to discourage the males in this drastic way.

The female spotted hyena also appears to grow a penis. She too develops an enlarged clitoris, which is exactly the same size and shape as the male penis, and also matches it for rigidity. Bizarrely, she also urinates, mates and gives birth through this organ, as her vagina is fused shut. This often leads to painful tearing when giving birth, suffocating the firstborn cub, and killing one mother in ten. More generally, the female hyena's gender identity is unusual, since she is bigger and more aggressive than the males, and plays like a male while a juvenile.

The reason for this seems to be that the female hyena

needs to produce a lot of testosterone, because hyena society is very fierce. Hyenas fight with one another throughout their lives. They are usually born in pairs, and one twin will often kill the other. Furthermore, hyena society is extremely hierarchical, and the female's social status seems to be inherited, as high-ranking, aggressive females pass on their dominant personality to their male heirs.

Which tadpole changes shape to foil its predator?

There is a species of frog called *Rana pirica*, whose tadpoles have evolved a unique way of protecting themselves from predators. The tadpoles can sense whether or not their predators, which are salamander larvae, are nearby. If the tadpoles sense the presence of a predator, they transform themselves into a different, bulging body shape, which makes them too big for the salamander larvae to fit into their mouths. Then, if the predators leave, the tadpoles will return to their normal size.

However, the salamander larvae have developed an equally impressive response, in what seems to be a fascinating evolutionary arms race. If they sense the presence of the *Rana pirica* tadpoles, the salamander larvae will also change their shape, with their heads becoming much broader, allowing them to swallow the enlarged tadpoles.

Which insect grows a model ant on its back?

Dangerous creatures tend to have distinctive markings, because it is important that they be recognised as dangerous. Honeybees, for example, carry a sting that can be deadly for many of their potential predators. However, if it is forced to actually use its sting, the bee itself will die. Therefore, the bee has a distinctive black and yellow pattern, colours that are understood in nature to indicate poison, so that its sting can serve as a deterrent. Similarly, the poison-dart frogs of the Amazon have incredibly lurid, colourful skins, which serve to warn predators that they are among the most poisonous creatures on the planet.

However, if this strategy proves to be effective, then it opens up the possibility of mimicry. If looking like a bee is enough to dissuade predators, then why should a creature actually bother to develop a poisonous sting, which costs considerable resources and energy? Thus, while bees, wasps and hornets are actually dangerous, there are also numerous other insects that look just like them, but which in fact carry no sting at all. For them, just looking dangerous is enough.

This mimicry is developed to an incredible degree by a small treehopper called *Heteronotus*, which is found in the forests of Central America. This amazing bug has evolved a full-scale model of an ant, which it wears on its back. If you look at it from above, as a bird would, all you will see is the black shape of an ant, with gaping jaws, a thin waist and a black abdomen. However, beneath this amazing imitation is the treehopper itself, which has a normal treehopper abdomen and wings, and looks in all other respects just like an average member of its family. Looking like an ant protects the treehopper from birds, because birds generally avoid eating ants, because they taste awful, they have a hard exoskeleton, and they often sting or bite.

Do snakes fart?

Snakes have a number of ways of scaring off potential predators. They will hiss at them, raise themselves up, puff up their bodies or rattle their tails. However, there are two types of North American snake which have another, rather unusual way of scaring off their enemies. The Sonoran coral snake and the Western hooknose snake are both quite small, which makes it harder for them to be physically imposing. Instead, they fart, although the technical term is the rather more genteel 'cloacal popping'. Each 'pop' lasts for less than two-tenths of a second, and may be repeated several times. Relative to the snake's size, these farts are quite loud: they can be heard up to 2 metres (6.5 feet) away, and they are said to sound just like human farts, but slightly higher pitched.

In fact, the volume of the farts may be

why they are effective: because they sound like the farts of larger animals, this may be enough to scare off the snake's usual predators. In tests, the snakes were found to fart only when threatened. They do so using two sets of muscles, which isolate a compressed bubble of air, and then release it to the outside in an explosive burst. Apparently, they sometimes put so much force into these farts that they fling themselves up off the ground!

Why do cats all look so similar, when dogs are so diverse?

It's true that domestic cats all look fairly similar to one another, in comparison with dogs, but there are cats that are more diverse and varied, such as lions, tigers, leopards, jaguars and ocelots. However, these are actually different species from our domestic cat, whereas all the strange and wonderful breeds of dog are all part of the same species: *Canis lupus familiaris*. Different breeds of the domestic cat, *Felis catus*, do look somewhat different – some have long hair, some have short hair, some are patterned, some are thin, some are heavy, and so on. However, the various breeds of domestic dog, including St Bernards, Dalmatians, poodles, greyhounds, chihuahuas, and so on, are far more varied than cats.

There are a number of reasons for this. Dogs have historically been much more useful for human beings than cats have. Dogs can be easily trained, and can be used for hunting, guard duty, shepherding, and many other tasks.

Cats, on the other hand, are only really useful for keeping mice away from crops, or as a pet. As a result, dogs have been domesticated and actively bred since around 15,000 BC, on three continents: Europe, Asia and Africa. Cats, on the other hand, were probably first domesticated in around 7,500 BC, in the Middle East, where farming originated.

Because dogs were bred on a number of continents, certain differences would have naturally evolved. Some would have become bigger, some would have developed thicker coats, some would have developed speed for hunting, and so on. In the last few hundred years, humans have taken a more active role, deliberately breeding dogs to produce offspring that are better suited for a particular job. Speedy dogs would be paired up, to produce extra-fast hunters. Big dogs would mate together, producing bigger guard dogs, and so on.

Furthermore, it seems that dogs are particularly well suited to this kind of selective breeding. In recent years, scientists have finished mapping the DNA of dogs, the Dog Genome Project. By analysing the genetic code of the domestic dog, geneticists have found that the genes that control growth in dogs are relatively simple, can be passed down easily, and reinforce one another strongly, which means that breeding dogs of a particular size will have a substantial effect on the size of the offspring.

Why do zebras have stripes?

The reason why zebras have their distinctive stripes is one of nature's most enduring mysteries. Even today we are still not sure exactly why such an unusual feature should have evolved, although a number of theories have been proposed. One long-standing theory holds that this pattern works as camouflage, breaking up the outline of the zebra on the open savannahs of Africa, where it roams. Many scientists are far from convinced by this, for the simple reason that zebras are quite conspicuous, and do not seem to be well camouflaged at all. However, the zebra's main predator is the lion, which is colour-blind, so it is possible that the zebra's vertical stripes do camouflage it in tall grass, even though to our eyes its coloration may make it appear conspicuous.

Another theory suggests that the zebra's alternating bands of black and white stripes reflect heat in different ways, creating cooling currents of air over the zebra's body. Yet another proposes that the stripes confuse the visual system of the bloodsucking tsetse fly. However, at least one function does seem to have been convincingly demonstrated. Zebras' stripes vary significantly from one individual animal to another, and it's clear that zebras do identify and recognise other members of the group by these distinctive markings.

Index

accents, bird 11–12
adder 129
African lungfish 172
afterbirth 34–5
alarm calls 64–6
alcohol consumption 97
Alcon Blue 79–80
algae 132
Amazon rainforest 65, 92, 96, 164,
    206–7
anglerfish 60–1, 147–8
anteaters 102–3
antechinus 157
antifreeze 17–18
ants 73–4, 79, 86, 87
    and anteaters 102–3
    anting 127–8
    Dracula 50–1
    driver 173–4
    farming 26–7
    model 206–7
    pharaoh 123–4
antshrike 65
apes 126–7
    see also specific species
aphid farms 26–7
aplomado falcon 133
archer fish 167–8
Arctic woolly bear caterpillar 17
armadillo 172
Asian blue-throated bee-eater 40
Atures 15–16

babirusa 129
baboons 109
badgers 70–1, 126–7
bass fish 37
Batrachochytrium dendrobatidis 31
bats 4–5, 126
bears 172
beavers 7–9, 134
bees 70–3, 86, 206
bioluminescence 56
birds of prey 39–40, 112–14, 132,
    156, 176–7
birdsong 11–12, 64–5, 66–8
black jewel beetle 93–4
blackbird 12
blister beetle 72–3
blood-drinkers 187–9
boobies 187–8
Boran bushmen 71
Boulengerula taitanus 32–3
box jellyfish 164
brain size 99–101, 106–7
burials 11
butterflies 79–80, 156, 199

caecilians 32–3
camels 172
camouflage 13–14, 57, 59, 63, 116,
    132, 156, 191–2, 195, 197–8, 210
cancer 14–15
cannibalism 32–3, 50–1, 140–2
capuchin monkey 66

catfish 23–4
cats 87, 98–9, 106–7, 126–7, 208–9
cattle 4, 87, 96–7, 108, 115–16, 118–22
cerebral cortex 101
chaffinch 11–12
chameleons 13–14
chickens 66, 108, 194
chicks 44, 49–50
chimpanzee 95–6, 109, 126
civet 28–9
clothes moths 113
cockroaches 12–13, 86, 172–3
coelacanths 192–3
collared flycatcher 200, 201
common tern 82
cone shell 164
coot 43–4
Cordyceps 27
coyote 64
cranes 117–18
crocodiles 83, 162–4
cross-dressing, animal 80–2
crows 61–2, 90, 127
cuckoo 49–50
currawong 76–7
cuttlefish 13–14, 80–1
cutworm moth 58
Cyclosa mulmeinensis 59–60

dam building 7–8
damselfish 2
Darwin, Charles 152, 187
deception 47–8, 64–6, 77–82
decoys 59–60
depression 84–6
dermatotrophy 33
dermestid beetle 9–10
detectives, reptilian 10–11
digger bees 72–3
dinosaurs 193–4
Dog Genome Project 209
dogs 5, 14–15, 85, 106–7, 126–7, 133–4, 208–9
dolphins 108, 181–3

drug-taking 96–7
dung beetles 68, 202–3
dunnock 158–9

eagles 39, 132, 176–7
earthquake prediction 23–4
earthworms 2–3, 4, 55–6
eels 37–9
eggs
    egg-eating 62
    hiding 47–8
    incubation 35–6, 41
    reptilian 51–2
Egyptian vulture 62
electromagnetism 24
elephants 4, 94–5, 99–100, 105–6, 108, 175–6
elvers 38
encephalisation quotient (EQ) 106–7
esca 148
Eurasian oystercatcher 157–8
evergreen forest warbler 22
exoskeletons 124
extinction 83, 152
eye gnat 122
eyesight 18–20, 104, 155–6, 197–8

face flies 121–2
fairy wren 76–7, 146–7
farting 118–20, 207–8
ferret 85–6
field of vision 155–6
fieldfare 177–8
fireflies 56
fishing 69–70, 148
flatworms 3, 138
fleas 126–7
forensic entomology 9–10
forest fires 93–4
fossa 203–4
freezing temperatures 17–18
frigate bird 132–3
frogs 135–6, 205
    common rain 155

false heads 200
frozen 17–18
glass 201–2
poison-dart 92, 164, 206
pregnancy tests 29–31
reproduction 154–5
skin-eating 135–6
South African clawed 30–1
vomiting 110
fulmar 114
fungi 27, 31
fungus gnat 93

Galápagos Islands 152–3, 187
Ganges River 11
gapes 49–50
gas companies 18–20
gauchos 57–8
giant panda 102
giant squid 166–7
Gila monster 120–1
gizzards 104–5
glass lizard 54–5
glial cells 100
global warming 83–4, 118–20
golden-headed cisticola 22
Gordian worm 86
gorillas 109
great grey shrike 153–4
great tit 200–1
green-tailed towhee 64
grief 108–9
grit-eating 104–5
ground squirrels 17, 45–6
grudge-bearing 175–6

Hannibal 3–4
harpy eagle 176–7
hedgehog 128–9
hermaphrodites 138, 139
hermit crab 179
herons 69–70, 118
hibernation 17–18
histolysis 93
honeydew 26

honeyguide 70–1
hornbill 115
horse 3, 108
hyenas
    brown 130
    spotted 204–5
Hymenoepimecis argyraphaga 170–1
hypnotism 75–6, 155–6

incest 146–7
infanticide 36–7, 41–2
injury-feigning 62–3
intelligence 99–101, 106–7, 125–6

jaguar 98, 172, 208
jay 127

kangaroos 95, 120
kidnapping 181–2
killer whale 53, 195
kingfishers 115
kraken 166

lancet liver fluke 87
lapwing 62–3
larders 7–9, 56
learning 107
lemmings 88–9, 134
leopard 208
linnet 49
lion 98, 208, 210
lionfish 1–2
little boxer crab 179
little egret 69–70
`living fossils' 193
lobster 124, 150
locoweed 96–7
Lonesome George 152–3
lyrebird 66–8

macaw 96
magpie 177–8
mantis shrimp 178–9
Maypures 16
medicine 95–6

megapodes 35–6
mermaid's purses 21
Mesonychoteuthis hamiltoni 167
metamorphosis 93
methane 119, 120
mice 30, 86–7, 105–6, 113
    grasshopper 185
migration 91
mimicry 66–8, 72–4, 206
mites 159
mockingbird 175
mole 55–6
monitor lizard 52
mosquitoes 165
muggers 132–3
muskrat 9

nacunda nighthawk 115–16
naked mole rat 198–9
nests 47–8, 149–50
    decoration 111–12
    decoy 76–7
    destruction 41
    ground 62–4
    sewing/weaving 21–3
neurons 100
nutcracking 61–2

ocelot 208
octopuses 191–2
    algae 192
    blanket 145–6
    coconut 192
    common 86
    mimic 1–2
ostrich 104–5
owls
    burrowing 68
    pellets 112–13
oxpecker 188–9

parasites 86–7, 126–7, 188–9
parenthood 32–53, 86
parrots 84–5, 96
parthenogenesis 73

pedipalps 143–4, 161
Penduline tit 47–8
penguins 53, 114–15, 195–6
    Adélie 149–50
    macaroni 39–40
penises
    penis fencing 138
    penis-eating 140, 143–4
    phony 204
    see also pedipalps
pheromones 58, 72, 79–80, 82, 139,
    148, 156
pigeons 6–7, 13
pigs 4, 37, 108, 125–6, 126–7, 129
pinacate (stink) beetle 184–5
planarians 3
Plesiometa argyra 170–1
plover 62–3
poisonous animals 92, 121, 164, 189,
    200, 206
    immunity to 128, 145
Pokomo tribe 163–4
polyembryony 93
poo 111–12, 114–17, 131, 133–5,
    202–3
pornography 101–2
Portuguese man o' war 145
potoo 197–8
praying mantis 140–2
predator avoidance 2, 45–6, 54–5,
    57, 62–4, 76–7, 111–12, 115–16,
    132–3, 135, 179, 195, 197–200,
    205–7, 210
pregnancy tests 29–31
present-giving 179–81
problem solving 107
promenade à deux 151
promiscuity 146–7
prostitution 149–50
Pseudoceros bifurcens 138
purple sandpiper 63–4
purple-throated hummingbird 149
pythons 191

quails 151–2

INDEX

rabbit 75–6, 94–5, 126, 134
rainbow pitta 111–12
Rana pirica 205
rape 181–2
ratel (honey badger) 70–1
rats 13, 86–7, 126, 127
remote-control animals 12–13
reproduction 21, 66–8, 73–4, 80–4,
    91, 94, 109, 137, 138–61, 179–83,
    186
rescue work 13
resilient creatures 171–3
rhesus macaque 101–2
rhino 104, 131
ruminants 118–20

sagebush cricket 159–60
salamanders 18, 205
scarab beetles 172
scorpions 18, 150–1
scrub-jay 136–7
sea anemone 179
sea lion 6
secretary bird 168–9
seet calls 64–5
sentinel systems 64–6
sewing birds 21–3
sharks 13, 182
    knot tying 20–1
    sand tiger 42–3
    turning upside down 99
sheep 74–5, 96, 108, 118–20
shingleback lizard 109, 199
shrike tanager 65
sibling killing 39–40, 42–3
side-blotched lizard 142–3
skinks 54
sloth 131–2, 176–7
slugs 139–40
smell, sense of 18–20
smoky tetanolita 58
snails 87
snakes 129
    brown tree 111–12
    garter 81–2

prey swallowing 189–91
rattlesnakes 77–8
sea 1, 2
Sonoran coral 207–8
Western hooknose 207–8
sociable weaver 22–3
social isolation 84–5
sole 1, 2
sparrows 22, 41–2
spiders 86, 143–4, 165–6, 170–1
    Australian social 53
    bird-dropping 57
    bolas 57–8
    European crab 160–1
    funnel-web 164
    hackled orb-weaver 166
    nursery web 180
    orb 59–60, 161, 166
    present-giving 179–81
    redback 181
    tent cobweb weaver 144
    underwater (diving bell) 24–6
spider's webs 59–60
spitting cobra 164
squirrels 17, 45–6, 77–8
starling 127
starvation 94–5
stick insects 73–4
stoat 63, 75–6
storks 117–18
stress 84–6, 199
suicide 86–9

tail-shedding 54–5
tailor bird 22
tardigrade 163
teeth 94–5
temperature regulation 17–18,
    117–18, 120–1, 142–3, 196, 219
termites 51–2, 86, 103, 174
territorial marking 130–1
testes 147–8
tiger 98, 208
toads 128, 136
    European midwife 46–7

exploding 89–90
Surinam 44–5
tonic immobility 99
tortoises 128, 152–3
Toxoplasma gondii 86–7
treehoppers 206–7
tsunamis 24
turtles
green 91
snapping 10–11, 60–1
tusks 129

urination 150–1
urohydrosis 117

vampire finch 187–9
velvet worm 185–6

vervet monkey 65–6, 97
violence, random 182–3
vomiting 110, 112–14, 132–3
vultures 18–20, 62, 117, 194–5

warfare 3–7
wasps 51, 59–60, 170–1
ichneumon 80
weaving birds 22–3
whales 53, 99–100
white-winged chough 169–70
woodpeckers 196–7

yellow-rumped thornbill 77

zebra 210